Mary Lou's and Dinah's book should  every actor before they even get to L. of it in my waiting room.

G. CHARL
Casting Director, *That 70's Show*

Everything you need to know is in this book!

KELLY ROWLAND,
Destiny's Child

Read this book or I won't cast you.

NANCYLEE MYATT,
Executive Producer, *South of Nowhere*

At last! A book that treats the young actor as an artist and craftsman, without sacrificing any of the fun to be had along the way!

TONY SHALHOUB,
Emmy Award–winning star of *Monk*

This clear and simple guide to acting is a must-have!

CATHERINE MACNEAL,
Lisa Taylor on *100 Deeds for Eddie McDowd*

In the lightning pace of television there is little time to stop and teach leaving most actors adrift. Mary Lou and Dinah can't always be there but their *book* can.

VALERIE LANDSBURG,
Director/Actress, one of the
original stars of the series *Fame*

Fantastic and well-needed addition to the young actor scene. This covers all the bases!

No amount of money is worth the effort unless it comes from the love of what you do. *Acting For Young Actors*...puts the LOVE first!

The most comprehensive guide for young actors so far!

A must for any young actor! An unbeatable resource packed with great advice from experienced professionals.

You won't believe how much is crammed into this one guide— it's a super source!

Acting is a very rewarding and fun experience. This book gives some great information on how to accomplish your goals and become the actor you've always wanted to be.

ACTING
for Young Actors

ACTING
for Young Actors

The Ultimate Teen Guide

Mary Lou Belli & Dinah Lenney

Back Stage Books/New York

Senior Editor: Mark Glubke
Editor: Cathy Hennessy

Text copyright © 2006 by Mary Lou Belli and Dinah Lenney

Published in 2006 by Back Stage Books,
an imprint of Watson-Guptill Publishing Group,
a division of the Crown Publishing Group,
Random House, Inc., New York
www.crownpublishing.com
www.watsonguptil.com

Library of Congress Cataloging-in-Publication Data to come

ISBN-13: 978-0-8230-4947-9
ISBN: 0-8230-4947-7

Printed in the U.S.A.

First printing, 2006

7 8 9 / 14 13 12

I dedicate this book to three generations of actors: For Edith, who has conducted her life and career with the conviction that acting is a noble profession. For Kitty and Suanne, whose guidance has helped so many young actors soar! For Tim and Maggie, whose work and exploration have only begun.

MARY LOU BELLI

For my students, who continue to teach me the things I forgot I knew and then some.

DINAH LENNEY

Contents

Foreword

When I was asked to write an introduction for this book, I immediately said "yes." Then I started to get really nervous. Because the truth of the matter is, I have no idea how to write an introduction. I know what I care about, but the thought of sharing it with people I don't know is frightening to me. But I have a little rule for myself: If something scares me, I force myself to face it. (Unless it's a guy who wants to fight me for no reason. Then I run. Fast.) I remember one of the most freeing moments in my life was when I was in high school and I made a firm decision to stop trying so hard to be "cool." It seemed to me that in order to be "cool" you had to pretend like you didn't care about anything, and that was just not working for me. In hindsight, I don't know why I was so desperate to be "cool," but it was important to me at the time. I'm easily excited, though, so it was hard for me to pretend like I'm not interested in anything life has to offer. One day, I was listening to the radio and "Hey Jude" by The Beatles came on. In the middle of it, Paul McCartney sings, "For well you know that it's a fool who plays it cool, by making his world a little colder." Hearing that lyric, I had an epiphany: Why am I trying so hard to make people like me by pretending

xiv ACTING FOR YOUNG ACTORS

I'm someone I'm not? Why don't I be as passionate about everything as I want to be, and stop worrying so much? From that point on, I was weird when I wanted to be weird, I was excited when I wanted to be excited, and I danced how I wanted to dance, and people stared, and probably made fun of me, but the great thing was I didn't care! I was being true to myself and having fun! So anytime I'm scared of something, I know it's that lingering part of my ego that still wants everyone to think I'm cool, and is scared of being embarrassed. The truth is, I'd rather fall on my face having tried something that scares me than never know what could have been. So here I am, and I'll just talk about a couple of things that have proved valuable to me along the way.

While I was studying at the Atlantic Theater Company, one of my teachers, an amazing woman named Karen Kohlhaas, had us all sit down one day and take fifteen minutes to write out what we wanted to say with our work. We were a little confused at first, mostly because nobody had ever asked that of us before, but it turned out everybody had something unique to say. I ended up copying my "mission statement" down in a book, and anytime I feel like I don't know what I'm doing or why I'm doing it, I can read it again and remind myself. It's something that's mine and only mine, a secret that colors all of the work I want to do and gives me permission to respect myself. It makes me feel valid as an artist, at least in purpose. It gives me something to fight for, something to stand behind, something to be proud of. Sometimes when I'm working on something I can begin to feel like I am expected to follow everyone else's vision. Only recently have I been able to stand up for myself if something doesn't feel right to me, and I feel this is largely because I feel like I'm fighting for something larger than myself.

The point is, everybody has something to say and a unique voice with which to say it. No one has had the experiences you've had so far but you. What do you have to say for yourself? Why is it important for anyone to hear? I've been told that one of the many purposes of art is to make people feel less alone. There are performances I've seen where an actor has done something so familiar to me that I feel as if they must know me. Who can say how many people will be affected by what you and only you have to offer?

It's important to educate yourself to the best of your abilities. Every once in a while some young person would come up to my dad, having recognized him as a working actor, and ask him for advice about what they could do to become actors themselves. My dad would invariably say, "Read two plays a day." This response usually invoked some quizzical looks from the young people, mainly because what they were really asking was, "How and when can I get famous?" which is a different question altogether. The fact is, if you want to be an actor, the more you know about the history of your art, the better. Actually, the more you know about everything the better. That's one of the beautiful things about acting. Everything is research!

If you decide you want to act professionally, try to stay focused on the things you love about acting. Don't let the business element poison you. It's this poison that makes people start talking about other human beings as "connections," for example. There's a business side to things of course, but not to the exclusion of your humanity and creativity. And what about working on the core before focusing on the fluff? It's easy to get caught up in the business world, but it's actually a disconnect to the art of acting. And by the way, I have never met a "connection." I don't believe they exist. I know people who have earned a level of mutual respect, but I guarantee you, if you go out in search of "connections" you won't find a single one. In fact, every time you say, "I do believe in 'connections,'" a little "connection" somewhere falls down dead.

Instead, start looking around you. Find your unique voice and use it. Keep your eyes peeled for people who inspire you, and most importantly, live your life. Some people get so caught up in it all that they lose touch with what's real, and they end up limiting themselves. For the most part, the characters you will be auditioning for and playing will not be show-business-obsessed, self-absorbed actors, so try to remain as grounded in the real world as possible. The friends that you make now can be invaluable to you later: As the respected anthropologist Margaret Mead said, "Never doubt that a small group of thoughtful, committed citizens can change the world; indeed, it's the only thing that ever has."

If you haven't yet had one of those teachers who sets you on fire with their passion for whatever it is they teach, do your best to seek one out. There is no better inspiration than learning from a person who is so passionate about what she loves that she has dedicated part of her life to share her knowledge with others.

One last thing: Beware of bitterness. In my experience, bitterness is something that creeps in at the edges of our personalities, at our weakest places—in our fears for the future, our self-doubt, our feelings of unworthiness, or inadequacy, into any of those places that we all have, as small or large as they might be—and slowly eats away at the artist in all of us by telling us that whatever we are doing in our lives is not good enough. It makes us obsessed with the unartistic aspects of show business, removes us from the reasons we initially became artists, and instills in us a hunger that can never be satiated. We begin determining our worth within as arbitrary and meaningless a hierarchy as the one Hollywood sets up for us. You and I both know that a person who is in a lot of magazines is not any more important than a person who has never been in one. But bitterness has the power to make people forget that. My hunch is that this type of bitterness especially infects people who set out to be celebrities, only to have their dreams unrealized, whereas people who strive to be artists are truly happy to be able to pursue their art. So many people other than you are in charge of whether or not you become a celebrity. But you and nobody else is in charge of the kind of artist you want to become.

Enjoy the rest of the book! You're in good hands.

JASON RITTER

Acknowledgments

Thanks to Mark Glubke, Cathy Hennessy, Charles Dougherty, Fred Mills, Robbie Kass, Kate Zentall, Jim Beaver, Joao Fernandes, Daphne Boelsma, Catherine MacNeal, Claudette Sutherland, Diana Wagman, Ellen Slezak, Hallie Freidman, and especially to all our contributors.

Introduction

Acting for Young Actors is for you. Everything you need to know about the craft and the business of acting, too—all in one book. Here, finally, is a realistic approach to the questions working actors ask themselves every time they play a part. *Acting for Young Actors* uses scenes from plays, movies, musicals, and television to teach you how to be a better actor. It introduces an actor's vocabulary and provides exercises to help you hone your skills. It gives you tips from professionals, and suggests further reading and viewing if you're hungry for more. Think of this book as a map, a practical guide, for doing what you already love to do even better. The point is to point the way to your acting dream, whether or not you intend to pursue it professionally.

Maybe you have an idea about what you want to do with your life, maybe you don't. Either way, if you love acting, you'll love this book. It's for those of you who are brave and uninhibited, and for those who are shy and self-conscious, too. We want to give you tools to access your imagination and your talent. With discipline and commitment, you'll gain confidence, overcome fear, and discover your unique gifts.

The truth is there's no substitute for good instincts, and nobody can teach you to be talented, but acting is a craft that can be learned and cultivated. Sanford Meisner, one of the pioneers of method acting and the founder of the Neighborhood Playhouse School of the Theatre in New York City, defined acting as "living truthfully under the given imaginary circumstances." If you're auditioning for a school play or starring in a television series, the measure of good acting is simple and the same: Does your audience believe you?

Credibility is only the beginning, though, and the rewards of deeper digging make the work more exciting for both you and the audience. It's one thing to transport us to an imagined reality, even better to learn to stretch, to tap your actor's intuition, to use your strengths and overcome your weaknesses to be the best actor you can be.

We present concrete ways for you to develop a character and to make informed and creative choices for that character based on research and intuition. Talking and listening are the keys to good acting, but they aren't enough by themselves. Your craft, to be specific and rich, should be based on what we'll call the five W's: Who, What, Why, Where and When. For every character you play, you need to answer these five questions:

1   Who am I?

2   What do I want?

3   Why do I want it?

4   Where am I?

5   When does this event take place?

We break down each of these questions and provide exercises to help you access the answers, to keep your instrument, your imagination, and your impulses limber and well-tuned when you're in the process of investigating a part. We discuss improvisation as it relates to creating a role and telling a story, but this isn't a book about creative dramatics or theatre games. Instead we emphasize strategies for working with scripted material, getting parts, and playing them fully. We offer suggestions about auditioning and we share our approach to monologues including information on where to find them and how to choose one that best shows you off. We explore the differences between acting for the camera and acting for a live audience and the merits of professional as opposed to on-the-job training. We suggest books to consult, plays to read, and movies to see. Included are resources to help you with the business of acting; from dealing with agents and casting directors to acquiring work permits and joining the unions. It's not our goal to make you a star. We aim to provide you with a practical approach to the craft of acting. This is a handbook, a guide to laying a solid foundation on which you can build a long, interesting, and rewarding career.

Especially today, when reality television is so popular, we want you to understand the difference between actors and celebrities; between *acting* and *behaving* under manipulated and extraordinary circumstances; between mannered or precocious behavior—which always rings false—and skilled, nuanced performance, which always rings true.

We want you to know how to make the most of rehearsal time whether you're in a school play or blocking a scene for camera on a movie set. And we want you to understand how time constraints in television and film sometimes limit rehearsal time and often demand you prepare a role before you ever get on a set.

Hopefully, you'll read this book over and over, turning down the corners of the pages and coming back to those places again and again, not just for information but for inspiration, too. Acting is a craft, but it's also a way of being, a way of living your life. The exploration of acting will lead you to a better understanding of yourself and other people. It will help make you a deeper, more tolerant, more well-rounded person whether you decide to act professionally or just for fun.

Chapter 1

Who Am I?

What's in a name?

You're a detective. Your job is to discover your role. The first question is: "Who am I?" The answer to that question begins with your name. Just as you have a name chosen by your parents, your character has a name chosen by the playwright. Whether it's Joan or Bob or Saint Joan or Sponge Bob, that name is your first clue to discovering who you are.

But a name can't tell us everything about a person—haven't we all known people whose names don't suit them at all? So your name is only the beginning, especially if it's a famous name, like Romeo, for example, a name about which we all have ideas and associations. Someday, sometime, you'll get to create a role. You'll be the first and possibly the only actor to play the part, especially if you're working in television or film. Teleplays and movies—except for the occasional remake—are produced one time only with a single cast, but plays are revived again and again on repertory stages all over the world. As a stage actor, you're bound to play parts that have been performed by lots of other artists through history. So how do you make a part your own? It's the specific and individual choices that you make that create a character and no two actors will do any part exactly the same way. Nor should they. You bring yourself to every part you play—your intellect, your emotional range, your unique sense of humor, the way you speak and move, and your physical qualities. Juliet can be blonde or brunette, short or tall, but that's the least of it. You have to get to know a part as well as you can so that you can bring yourself to it. Learning a role is about research, instinct, and deliberate choices, too. Each choice you act, consciously or not, will make your Romeo or Juliet different from anybody else's. Your job is to be true to the character and true to yourself—that's how you make a part your own.

Say you've been cast as Joan of Arc. It's tempting to run out and rent every performance you can at your local video store. But first it's essential that you give yourself a chance to discover who you are in the role. Once you understand the lines and after you've been in rehearsal for a while, it's terrific to watch another actor play the same part, and absolutely fine to steal from another actor's performance. There's a saying in show business: "Steal from the best!" No two actors will do anything exactly the same way even if they try.

Since the character is the author's creation, it's essential that you begin from the script, by breaking it down. The first step is to note and analyze information in the text, which can be divided into three categories:

1 What the author tells you about the character in stage directions and parentheticals.

2 What the other characters say about the character in dialogue.

3 What the character tells you about himself from his dialogue or actions.

It's helpful to make a chart of this information using columns for each category; that way the information is easy to compare and contrast.

TIPS FROM THE PROS

The most important piece of advice I can give about the craft of acting, is to remember that the best thing you, the actor can bring to the character is yourself. You can bring what already exists inside you: your thoughts, feelings, attitudes, beliefs, and expectations about the world. Use them. These things are your assets—your software. With that in mind, have as many interests and experiences outside acting as you can. It's like having more programs on your computer and that makes you more valuable. The more you explore life, the more you will have to bring to your craft. That's what I love most about this career. It promotes a lifestyle that allows you to explore a vast range of interests.

BROOKE DENYSE, ACTRESS

Ask the Author First!

Often, but not always, you can find your first answers to "Who Am I?" in the *dramatis personae* or cast list, which usually appears in most plays after the title page. This is a list of all the characters in the piece. It tells you how the characters are related to one another and sometimes includes a physical description of each one. In Shakespeare's *Romeo and Juliet*, Romeo is described in the dramatis personae as "Romeo, son to Montague." Mercutio is the next character on the list. He's described as "Kinsman to the prince, and friend to Romeo." Many movie, television, and play scripts offer more description when a character first appears in the action.

Let's go back to Joan of Arc, first as she's portrayed in *Saint Joan*, one of George Bernard Shaw's most famous plays. As is often true in a script, we're introduced to Joan in Scene 1, when she makes her first entrance.

> Joan appears in the turret doorway. She is an able-bodied country girl of seventeen or eighteen, respectfully dressed in red, with an uncommon face: eyes very wide apart and bulging as they often do in very imaginative people, a long well-shaped nose with wide nostrils, a short upper lip, resolute but full-lipped mouth and handsome fighting chin. She comes eagerly to the table, delighted at having penetrated to Beaudricourt's presence at last, and full of hope as to the results. His scowl does not check or frighten her in the least. Her voice is normally a hearty coaxing voice, very confident, very appealing, very hard to resist.

Shaw has also written a long preface to the play, discussing specific aspects of the character in sections with titles like, "Joan's Voices and Visions," "Joan's Manliness and Militarism," "Joan's Good Looks," and "Joan's Immaturity and Ignorance." To get this much information from the playwright is wonderful and unusual. If you were cast in any role in Shaw's *Saint Joan*, you'd read all of it, of course, especially the section called "Joan Summed Up," where Shaw ends with saying, "She was very capable, a born boss."

And if you're playing Joan in this play, lucky you, the "Who I am according to the author" column of your "Who am I?" chart will be extensive, filled with adjectives like eager, resolute, confident, appealing, capable, and bossy. Maybe you don't look like Shaw's physical imagining of Joan. Don't let that deter you! You can play Joan with a snub nose and an overbite, if you've done enough research to understand her from the inside out.

But now let's discuss another version of the Joan of Arc story, *The Lark*, a play written by Jean Anouilh and adapted by Lillian

Hellman. All you learn from the cast list at the front of the script is who played the role of Joan (Julie Harris), and there's no description of any of the characters in the text. In this case, what should you do? Go to the library! Find out about Joan in historical books! Check out Mr. Shaw, of course, since you're bound to discover that he wrote a play about Joan of Arc, too.

After describing his characters at the outset, the author might tell you more in the stage directions or parentheticals. Sometimes these aren't the author's words at all, but rather staging from the first production, transcribed from the stage manager's original notes. It's worth reading all stage directions at least once. Then, go ahead and cross out anything that isn't helpful.

When you get a copy of the script, always look to see if the publisher has included commentary or reviews, another great source for information and inspiration. In the case of *The Lark*, the back cover of the Dramatists Play Service edition explains that in this version of the Joan of Arc story the authors have incorporated two viewpoints. First, Anouilh and Hellman portray the historical Joan, a woman who will be judged worthy of sainthood by posterity; second, they mean to inhabit Joan's imagination, to create the character from the inside out, showing us the "simple girl who became an inspired warrior."

Ask the Other Characters!

Even after you've gone through the whole play and know how the author sees your character, your investigation continues.

Hopefully you read the entire script before you were cast, but sometimes—especially in the case of television and film—it isn't available. If you haven't read the script, now that the role is yours, it's time. Next up to discover is what other characters in the story have to say about you. It's an opportunity to do something we don't usually get to do in real life, to eavesdrop on gossip about yourself.

But it is gossip, remember, so don't believe it all. Other characters are capable of lying! It's possible, too, that they're simply misinformed. It's your job to sift through gossip and opinion and figure out what's true. Keep this in mind: As the character, you may not know what someone has to say behind your back, but as a craftsman, an actor playing a role, this information is necessary and useful. Still, finding and sorting information isn't enough by itself. You have to interpret the clues. You have to know the material well enough to *read between the lines.*

Going back to Act 1 of *The Lark*, before Joan can accomplish her mission, she needs the help of Beaudricourt, a captain in the Dauphin's army (at that time in France the Dauphin was the closest thing to a king). As her military advocate and escort, Beaudicourt will eventually lead her to the Dauphin, but only after she makes a nuisance of herself. He accuses her of being greedy, crazy, and strange. List these three characteristics in the "Who I am according to others" column of your "Who am I?" chart. But remember that as a good detective, you still need to investigate further.

All of these observations are accurate from Beaudricourt's point of view. In preparing to play the role, Beaudricourt's opinion informs you in two ways: First, it shows how Joan is perceived by others. And from there you can extrapolate to an understanding of the real Joan. It's clear she must have been brave to persevere in spite of public opinion, and very clever to enlist Beaudricourt himself in accomplishing her goals. So from greedy, crazy and strange, you are able to translate that she was courageous, smart and determined.

Ask Yourself!

You can find the most revealing clues about your character in your own dialogue and actions—what you say and what you do. Even if you're lying! If you are, it's up to you as an actor to figure out why and then to justify those actions. Whether a character is lying or not, she reveals the most telling things about herself through her own words and actions. For example, Joan has a moment in *The Lark*, when she tells Charles, the future king, she is afraid:

Joan: I've been in danger every minute of the way, and every minute of the way I was frightened. I don't want to be beaten, I don't want pain, I don't want to die. I'm scared.

Charles: (*Softly*) What do you do when you get scared?

Joan: Act as if I wasn't. It's that simple. Try it. Say to yourself, yes, I am afraid. But it's nobody else's business, so go on, go on. And you go on.

So in the "Who am I?" chart, under the heading "Who I am according to me?" you'd list "scared." In her dialogue Joan has revealed that she's not as bold as she appears to be, that it isn't always easy for her to stand up for what she believes. But isn't that what courage is all about? To persevere in spite of fear? And isn't this internal conflict part of what makes Joan interesting and human—a role worth playing? This information—from Joan herself—allows the actress to create a layered performance, to explore not just the strength of her character's convictions, but her insecurities and weaknesses as well. A complex character has emerged from your simple chart. And when Joan chooses death at the end of the play, her actions speak louder than words ever could.

Research

Imagine you're Julia Roberts playing Erin Brockovich, Johnny Depp playing J.M. Barry, or Leonardo DiCaprio playing Howard Hughes. You can do lots of digging when you're playing characters from history or real life. The question is, do you want to? As an actor you can use the text of the screenplay to find your way in the story or you can dig around.

If you choose to research, do as much as will help you. How much is enough? Enough to fire your imagination. Enough to inspire you to behave in character. Enough to fill in the blanks. *Filling in the blanks* is providing yourself with information, actual or made up, that will help you to inhabit the role. At its simplest, it may come down to knowing what year you were born and where you grew up. At its most complex, it's giving your character secrets that only you will know.

Often, you'll want to fill in the blanks with things you have in common with the character. This is called *personalizing*. An actor might want to bring a prop or wear a piece of clothing or jewelry that makes her feel closer to the character she is creating. Of course it helps to find bits of the character in yourself and vice versa, which is why an item of clothing or jewelry from your own dresser can ground you in a role.

If you're playing a character similar to you in temperament and experience, you may only have to close your eyes for a minute to inhabit the part. But maybe you're intimidated by the idea of playing someone whose experience is dramatically different from your own. Some actors actually find it easier to play characters with whom they have nothing in common. They feel less exposed, less vulnerable, and consequently freer to imagine, to research, to play and to act. Either way, if your craft is solid, you have nothing to worry about. It's exciting to play characters in situations that are foreign to you, once you're equipped to substitute places, events, and relationships from your own life to summon up the appropriate emotional and physical behavior you need to truthfully play those parts.

Either way, even if you know this character better than you know yourself, you'll need to engage your imagination to keep your performance honest and fresh. Use whatever tools and clues work for you and throw away the rest. There's no recipe or prescription for how to approach a part; it's up to you to decide on a case-by-case basis.

When we coach actors for auditions, we see them at the very beginning of their process. It's uncanny how clear it is when an actor makes the transition from reading the lines to being the character. A person's face and carriage will change from role to role. An actor we know supplemented his income by working as a model for a well-known sculptor. The sculptor knew of the actor's rising success and saw all the work the actor did on stage and screen. Each time the actor came to the studio to pose, the sculptor would ask him to choose from his own repertoire and to "be in character." Although it was the same actor who posed for each new work, the faces looked entirely different in every bust. Eventually, the artist named the sculptures for each of the characters chosen, and not for the actor himself. The point is that every role will change the way you look and feel inside and out, affecting not just your hair and make-up and wardrobe, but your posture and facial expressions, the way you speak and move, even the ways in which you are private and still.

Once you've played detective, and gathered as much information about your character as you can, you might want to assemble it all by writing an autobiography. Keep in mind that there are no rights and wrongs when creating a character. The idea is to get so comfortable in a role that you convince the audience that you're somebody else! It all starts with convincing yourself—and only you can judge how far you need to go to accomplish that goal.

TIPS FROM THE PROS

My advice? Learn everything. Don't limit yourself to acting classes. If you're determined to be an artist, you must know about all the arts. Look at paintings, read novels, dance, and sing. Acting isn't about getting on television or being in *People* magazine. It's an ancient profession with a tremendous amount of history. It's an actor's responsibility to read plays, to watch older films, to know about the famous performances of the past. In other words, you can't call yourself an actor or an artist if you have no idea what that means. Study.

ROSEMARY MORGAN,
AGE TWENTY-ONE, FOURTH GENERATION ACTOR

The craft of acting is the greatest way to truly get to know yourself. True actors cannot hide from their fears, phobias, issues, and blockages. Likewise, they cannot hide from their hearts, their feelings, their ideals, and their spirits. The process of becoming an actor may feel like therapy at times—but it is essential to uncover those unconscious beliefs and patterns that can keep us from living our true potential as artists, as communicators, and as people.

A reflective process and emotional outlet, acting allows you to explore, express, and examine your deepest feelings in a safe way. Because the art-form centers around "play," actors have unlimited freedom to reveal their imperfections in constructive ways.

KELLE MCQUINN, KIDTRIBE FOUNDER

ACTING EXERCISE:
Getting in Character

 Choose a character that you are familiar with from a play you've read, or a movie or TV show you've watched. Assume you *are* that character. Find a scene partner and ask him to interview you. Answer all his questions in the first person. Think of the character as yourself. If the interviewer asks: "Who are you?" You answer, " My name is … "

RECOMMENDED READING

Playing Joan by Holly Hill, Theatre Communications Group, 1987. This is a fascinating series of interviews with actresses who have all played the role of Joan of Arc. Each of them discusses how she approached the part, how it affected her, changed her, and made her a better actress.

RECOMMENDED VIEWING

Joan of Arc, starring Leelee Sobieski, is a miniseries that looks at Joan as a daughter, friend, leader, and woman. Available through Netflix.com

Joan of Arcadia, Season 1, starring Amber Tamblyn, is an imaginative modern telling of the Joan of Arc story set in present day California featuring Joan as a high school student who talks to God. Both Ms. Tamblyn and the supporting cast are exquisite in their roles. Available through Netflix.com.

Erin Brockovich, starring Julia Roberts. An example of a film about a real person where actual photographs and footage of the real Erin Brockovich are available for you to compare with Robert's portrayal of the role. Available through Netflix.com or at your local video store.

Chapter 2

What Do I Want?

Objectives and Intentions

Finding out who you are goes hand in hand with figuring out what you want and how you're going to get it. It's one of those existential questions, like which came first, the chicken or the egg. Knowing who you are will help you to figure out what you want, which will in turn enrich your understanding of who you are in the role.

You're going to hear actors and acting teachers use the words intention and objective when they talk about the craft of acting. These words have to do with finding the actions in a scene, which you cannot do unless you know what you want. Here's our best explanation: The *objective* is what you want. You achieve your objective by playing intentions or actions. **Actions** and *intentions* can always be expressed with verbs.

Be careful about answering the question: What do I want? It's seems easy enough but most actors bumble it by complicating the answer in spite of themselves. Actors forget that what they want— their objectives—are usually quite simple. A guy we know, we'll call him Joe, was rehearsing a scene from *The Dead Poets Society* (written by Tom Schulman), a film about a group of boys at a New England boarding school and their inspirational teacher. In the scene, Joe, who's playing Neil, tells his roommate that he knows what he wants for the very first time in his life; he wants to win a part in the school play. We asked Joe some questions to help him find his objective.

Authors: What do you want in this scene?

Joe: I want to audition for the school play.

Authors: True. What else?

Joe: I want to get the part?

Authors: Absolutely. What else?

Joe: I'm not sure...

Joe's answers weren't wrong, he got them straight out of the script. But Joe will have more to play if he considers not just the plot, but also his relationship with his scene partner. To be active and interesting, the answer to "What do I want?" needs to involve getting something from the other guy. What does Joe want from Brandon, his scene partner? To make him angry? To enlist his sympathy? To hurt him? To help him? All of those are objectives worth playing.

Joe shouldn't be afraid to try the scene multiple times, changing his objective with each rehearsal. In that way he'll find the choice that best serves him and discover how it affects the scene as a whole. Acting is dynamic not static, so every change Joe makes will have a domino effect. And that's good. It will make every moment in the scene fresh and new.

Show, Don't Tell

Anyone can tell a story! Anyone can read out loud! And anyone can regurgitate the plot! But telling isn't acting. You can tell the plot, but you can't act it! Here's a big hint: You won't go wrong if you remember what you are! You're an *actor*!

Determining what you want as an *actor* has to do with *act*ion, and it's your job to understand what you can act and what you can't. *Acting is doing.* Verbs are the answer every time; finding the verb to play is the key to getting what you want. But deciding what you want in the scene is just the beginning. The next step is figuring out how you are going to get it. It's like life! For example, there are lots of ways to get out of doing the dishes after dinner. Let's say your line is "Mom, I don't want to do the dishes tonight." How many ways are there to say that line? You can plead. You can insist. You can tease. You can have a breakdown. You can sing the line or shout it or whisper it or simply state it as a matter of fact. Notice that we suggested how to do this by using verbs: to plead, to insist, to tease, etc. The way you say the line depends on what you want and how you're going to try to get it. The more specific you are about what you want, the stronger your motivation to figure out how to get it, the more compelling it is to change your strategy when it isn't working. After all, just because you don't want to do the dishes doesn't mean you're going to get out of doing them. Remember achieving an objective in a scene is not the measure of the usefulness of that objective!

Back to Joe, who is still trying to determine his objective in that scene from *The Dead Poets Society*. The script tells us Joe wants to win a part in the school play. But those are circumstances, and not inherently dramatic—or actable—in and of themselves. Joe needs to find something to act, something not directly stated in the scene, something to go after that will make the scene jump off the page.

Authors: What do you want, Joe? Think about your partner in the scene. What do you want from him?

Joe: I want to tell him that I want the part?

Authors: Aha... Getting warm...

Joe: I want to tell him that I want to be an actor!

Authors: Okay. But how can we make that more exciting, more fun to do (to act, that is)? Choose a better verb to play. Don't just tell him, do something to him. What do you want to DO?

Joe: I want to convince him that it's a good idea!

Authors: Yes! Good! Convince is a good word. Go on...

Joe: I want him to take my side.

Authors: In what way?

Joe: I want him to get excited.

Authors: Even better. So how will you do that? What actions will you choose?

By the end of the hour, Joe has discovered that there are lots of ways to try to get what he wants. He can shout, he can jump up and down, he can whine, tease, wheedle and needle in his effort to get the desired response. And as for his partner, played by another actor, a young man named Brandon, what he wants is simple, too. He wants to be left alone! Presto! Conflict! Drama! This is rich material for a couple of young actors and something worth watching for the audience.

TIPS FROM THE PROS

ACTeen believes that acting is action oriented, and emotions are the result of intentions successfully or unsuccessfully achieved.

An actor does not come on stage or on set to "feel an emotion." The actor ventures into a dramatic situation *to do something*. If the actor is successful at what he aims to accomplish, he is happy, fulfilled, or self-satisfied. If the actor is thwarted in his attempts, he is angry, frustrated, or upset. Emotions are the by-product, and in essence take care of themselves without any attempt by the actor to first manipulate them or "work them up."

Too often young actors struggle mightily to "feel something." Most of this is wasted effort. It results in what I call the "taking your own pulse" school of acting. As in: "Am I feeling it? Am I feeling it *now*?" The result is that actors spend too much time being preoccupied with their own "inner lives" and stop noticing and FOCUSING on what's going on around them, i.e. the other actor.

There is a reason why acting is also re-acting. An actor who feels the electric two-way giving and receiving is truly alive. This truthfulness, this "holding the mirror up to nature," happens when actors are playing intentions involving their fellow actors. Actors should choose intentions linked to other actors. "I need" or "I want" something from them. This "want" or specific goal creates a connection, and listening, true listening occurs.

RITA LITTON, DIRECTOR OF ACTEEN, NEW YORK, NY

ACTING EXERCISE:
Action!

This exercise is designed to help you use action words to play intentions. Take a simple declarative sentence like, "It's none of your business." Partner #1 chooses five actions (or verbs) for partner #2 to use when saying this line. The first action is "to boss." Partner #1 says the line " It's none of your business" as though he is giving an order. The four alternative choices might be: to beg, to insult, to insist, and to tease. Partner #1 tries out each one and then partner #2 takes a turn with all five intentions. Defining your actions this way and finding the verbs to play helps each actor discover various ways to get what he wants: to achieve his objective.

Substitution

Sometimes you have to make a *substitution* in order to pursue what you want in a scene. Substitution is an acting tool and is used in different ways by different teachers, beginning with Constantin Stanislavski, a Russian, and the father of modern acting technique. His methodology is fundamental to craft as taught in America by Stella Adler, Lee Strasberg, Uta Hagen, and Herbert Berghof. To act, you have to find the truth of your relationships and the truth of your objectives. If you understand these things in your head, as a reader, as a student of literature, you're only partially there. Actors have to make things personal for themselves. It isn't enough to understand a feeling or an emotion, you have to actually feel it! That's where substitution comes in.

In *The Dead Poets Society*, the character of Neil has a difficult relationship with his father. But suppose that in real life Joe has a wonderful life with his father. Supposing Joe's father, unlike the character's father, is completely supportive of Joe's desire to be an actor. Then Joe needs to find a substitution: He needs to plug in somebody else, someone specific who makes life tough for him.

Suppose nobody makes life tough for Joe and that all the adults in his life are supportive and helpful. Supposing he can't think of a single person who gets in the way of his getting what he wants! That means Joe has to be imaginative, he can't just pretend to have those feelings. If he does, the audience will feel that something is off. We won't know exactly what's missing, but we won't believe Joe unless he's done his homework.

So substitution is allowing something to stand in for something else; it's plugging in something familiar and real for something that's strange, in order to access your real feelings and responses. If you access your personal truth in this way you won't indicate. *Indicating* is pretending to feel something you don't and it makes for bad acting. It's showing rather than doing—yes, we know, we said "show, don't tell!"—but indicating is over-doing, or doing too much. So how much is enough? Substitution works like your conscience to keep you honest. If you're using substitution effectively, you're able to live truthfully, in character, under the imaginary circumstances.

The Magic "As if"

What if Joe wasn't doing a scene about wanting to be in the school play? Suppose, instead, the scene was about wanting to be a doctor, wanting to go to medical school. Does Joe want to be a doctor? No way! He wants to be an actor! So how is he going to talk about dying to go to medical school? He's going to make another kind of substitution: He's going to talk about being a doctor as if he were talking about being an actor! *As if* is a magical phrase for actors—it allows us to act rather than indicate, to invest our real feelings in our work, rendering it authentic and believable for the audience.

In fact, Joe has already used "as if" to help him in his work on the role of Neil. The character resents his father, but Joe doesn't know what that feels like. He does know what it felt like to despise his eighth grade geometry teacher who made him feel stupid and inadequate. He's acquainted with resentment—he knows what it is to meet resistance—all of us do. So he makes a specific substitution: He speaks about his father "as if" he is talking about Mr. Willoughby, his eighth grade math teacher. Suddenly he's angry in the appropriate way.

TIPS FROM THE PROS

Is the character you or are you the character? This question is at the heart of one of the most difficult arguments about acting. The followers of Lee Strasberg encourage actors to find experiences in their own lives that parallel the experiences of the character in order to find a personal truth. The followers of Stella Adler insist that the actor should enter the life of the character, not the other way around. Almost everyone comes down on one side or the other. The argument against Strasberg's method is that it takes you out of character. The argument against Adler's is that it's pretense, not truth. Who's right? They both are.

The trick is knowing when to use which technique. If you read a script and feel moved by it, you're home. Your imagination, experiences, and intellect have come together and connected you to the events or characters that the script describes. That's what you want. The rest is just choices.

What if you don't connect, or only connect partially? That's where the work comes in. If you don't respond to a moment in the script imagine: What it would be like? This is Stanislavski's Magic As-If. If your imagination goes to, "What would it be like if this happened to the character," you're in Stella's territory. If your imagination goes to, "What would I do if this happened to me," you're with Lee.

JOEL ASHER, DIRECTOR, PRODUCER, ACTING TEACHER

"As if" is wonderfully useful whether it helps you to discover what you want, or to understand your relationships in the scene you're playing. "As if" gives you permission to pretend. It's another way to magically trick the brain into substituting one reality for another.

Patti Moore was one of our students in Performance for the Camera, a week-long seminar in the summer programs sponsored by the University of California at Los Angeles in conjunction with US Performing Arts Camps. A drama major at Ithaca College, Patti remembers the first time substitution really made sense to her. She'd been asked to perform a Cole Porter song with "sensuality." The direction was intimidating at first, but Patti stumbled on the "as if" phrase all by herself and almost by accident. In the middle of her own rehearsal, she heard another student playing the stand-up bass. Just listening to the music relaxed her and filled her with desire; Patti loves the bass and plays it herself! She wanted badly to get her hands on her bass that very minute. It occurred to her then that she could sing the song from that emotional place, that her feelings about the bass were enough to emotionally launch her in just the right way. She would sing the song "as if" she were singing about that feeling—that desire. So simple and so effective! If you are specific in this way, if you come up with the right actions and the right substitutions, your work will be exciting and credible, not just for the audience but for yourself.

But here's a cautionary tale about an "as if" backfiring. A girl we know, Talia, auditioned to play a part in a TV pilot of a child with an obsessive-compulsive disorder (O.C.D.). In the audition scene, the character was supposed to spill water on her dress and freak out. Talia was seven at the time. It was no good to explain to her, or any actor of any age, the psychological manifestations of O.C.D. No amount of intellectual discussion could make the situation real for her. Instead, Talia had to imagine something personal that would make her very upset. She needed a magic "as if." During the coaching session we learned that Talia was afraid of spiders. When she pretended the cup of water was full of spiders she was able to play the scene believably. But later that day, at the audition, Talia's mother wasn't satisfied that Talia's hysteria was real enough. "Pretend I'm going away," the mother told her daughter. "Pretend you will never see me again." Sure enough Talia started to cry. The problem was, she couldn't stop. She may have been the best actress for the job, but she didn't get it.

An "as if" that is too emotionally hot for you may not be the best choice. If you're worried about losing control, use it cautiously in a safe rehearsal environment. On the other hand a hot "as if" may trigger a breakthrough because it accesses your emotional truth so well.

Conflict

In life, almost anything worth doing or worth having requires effort. The greatest rewards come when we overcome obstacles. We can't talk about going after your objective without addressing the existence and usefulness of obstacles. An **obstacle** is something that gets in your way. It stops you from achieving your objective. Obstacles can be physical or emotional. You can create them for yourself, or they can pre-exist in the text. In most cases, too, you're not alone in the scene. You've determined what you want, but so has the other guy. Bingo, more obstacles! We call this the **ying/yang** of conflict—the push and pull of the scene. If you look at the ying/yang symbol, you'll see that one side is the reciprocal or opposite of the other, so that when they are placed side by side they make a whole. You need the opposing objectives of two characters in a scene to create conflict. Conflict is what makes the work interesting. It's what makes the audience sit forward in their seats and want to watch. It's what brings a scene to life.

So how can you create conflict in a scene? You can't! Not all by yourself. You can only bring your strong objective and play your actions, and hope that the other actor in the scene does the same. If you're both working well, the conflict will naturally emerge.

During rehearsal, if your character is supposed to walk away or leave the room in a scene—do it! If your partner in the scene is supposed to stop you from leaving, it's his responsibility to keep you in the room. If you stay to have the scene, because the script says so, you're robbing your scene partner of the opportunity to play his objective. There won't be any conflict! If just one time you play the scene fully in rehearsal, exiting before you're supposed to, the next time your scene partner will come up with the goods—the intentions he needs—to keep you in the room!

Subtext

Have you ever overheard a conversation you weren't supposed to hear? Remember, if you can, how you weren't just listening but also thinking, feeling guilty perhaps, worrying about getting caught, maybe coming to conclusions of your own about what was being said. Your thoughts were your subtext. You always have one, whether you're speaking aloud or not. Even when you do speak, you don't always say exactly what you mean or mean exactly what you say, which is also true of every character you'll ever play. When you specify for yourself what a character is thinking between and under the lines, that's the *subtext*.

In another scene from *The Dead Poets Society*, Neil has a scene with his father, Dr. Perry, who's decided—without consulting Neil—that his son has too many extracurricular activities. His father says: "When you've finished medical school and you're on your own you can do as you please. Until then, you will do as I say. Is that clear? I said is that clear?" Neil nods. But what is he thinking? The next scene gives us a clue. Neil enters, slams his door and explodes, calling his father a bastard and a son-of-a-bitch. So what sort of subtext might Joe, in the role of Neil, try in rehearsal as he listens to the actor playing his father? He might think, "I hate you, you're ruining my life." only to find that self-pity doesn't inspire the anger he needs in the next scene. So he might try thinking, "I'll never do what you say as long as I live!" and immediately realize that sets up the determination that catapults him into the behavior he needs.

ACTING EXERCISE:
The Subtext

This exercise is designed to isolate your use of subtext and encourage you to notice the change it can make in a performance. Choose a partner and a simple declarative sentence. Let's use the same line from the last exercise: "It's none of your business." Partner #1 chooses five examples of subtext for partner #2 to use when saying this line. For example: You are such a jerk; I don't want you to know; Leave me alone; Please don't make me tell you; Get out of my face. After partner #2 tries to deliver the line acting each of the five subtexts, it's time to switch. While partner #1 is listening, she should be working on subtext, too. What does she think and feel in response to partner #2's intentions and subtext? She can experiment with different alternatives. Defining your subtext, whether you're speaking or not, feeds the emotional life of the character and makes your actions even more specific and interesting.

TIPS FROM THE PROS

When you memorize your lines, you have not finished your work. You need to activate your subtext. Good actors are always thinking when they are not speaking. So, what is going on in your mind between the lines? An actor who can keep his thoughts moving is an actor who is really listening and not just waiting for his turn to speak.

KATE BENTON, ACTING INSTRUCTOR AT
HARVARD WESTLAKE MIDDLE SCHOOL, LOS ANGELES

Putting It All Together

You've decided what you want (your objective) and how you are going to get it (your actions). You're thinking about substitutions and personalizations that will serve you in the part (your "as ifs") and you're beginning to investigate what the character is thinking under the lines (your subtext). How do you go about using all that in a scene? Here are the last four lines of the scene between Neil and Todd from *The Dead Poets Society*:

Todd: I can take care of myself just fine. Okay?

Neil: Er . . . No.

Todd: No? What do you mean "no?"

Neil: No.

Think of all the ways there are to play these lines! The first time Joe and Brandon do the scene they end up shouting at each other from beginning to end. By the time they've finished rehearsing, they've discovered other ways to get what they want based on character, objective, relationship, and subtext.

So many choices! All of them depending on who you are, what you want, and how you decide to get it. And that's the art of acting—the creativity and the craft—it's all in the choices and the choices are up to you!

RECOMMENDED READING

The Art of Acting by Stella Adler, Applause Books, 2000. Adler's book is divided into twenty-two classes. Each 'class' forms a chapter, and has a named subject as its organizing principle. ("Acting is Doing," "Developing the Imagination," "Building a Vocabulary of Actions," etc.) Great instruction from a master!

An Actor Prepares by Constantin Stanislavski, Routledge, 1936. Stanislavski was the first to treat acting as a craft, accessible through discipline and commitment to practice and exercise. Stanislavki's teaching is at the root of modern theatre training all over the world.

Chapter 3

Why Do I Want
What I Want?

Use Yourself

You know who you are! You know what you want! Now comes the most personal part of acting, the part where you get to really use yourself. Asking "why" is how you get to exercise not just your intellect, but also your imagination and your creativity. The question, "Why do I want what I want?" brings your character to life because it brings *you* to life.

Somebody once said that acting is like standing up naked and turning around slowly. The truth of it is, to act is much more revealing than just taking off your clothes. You're turning yourself inside out, showing us who you are on the inside and *why* you behave as you do. You couldn't be more vulnerable.

Have you ever felt as though you knew a character you saw on television? Famous actors are often approached in public because we get to feel as though we know them personally. But actors are sensitive about being identified with their characters. They'll

remind you that they're acting, that the characters aren't real.
They might even tell you they have nothing in common with the
role, and that could be absolutely true. Even so, it's the actor's
unique physical and emotional qualities—his instincts, feelings,
strengths, vulnerabilities, and humor—that make the character
someone you recognize and even love. No wonder people get
confused.

When there's a *why* behind your actions, a reason riding under
your objective, there's the possibility for conflict and
consequences. Something is **at stake**. The more personal and
specific your reasons, the more vulnerable you are, the more
truthful your performance. What makes it truthful? What makes
it compelling? You! The way your brain ticks, the way you
operate, the way you express emotion is what makes your acting
unique and moving. Once you hook yourself into your *why*, there
can be no separation between you and the character. Think of the
character as your vehicle—your car!—the way you think, feel, and
react is the fuel that drives the character forward.

In Arthur Miller's *The Crucible*, Abigail Williams is a liar, willing
to condemn innocent neighbors as witches in order to get what
she wants. And what does she want? She wants John Proctor, who
is married to somebody else. Why? Because she's in love with him!
When you're looking for answers to the question why, don't mess
around. Don't equivocate. The strongest reasons have to do with
love, hate, revenge, fear, jealousy, and power. Abigail is motivated
by love and revenge. To play this character you have to be willing
to tap into your own deep feelings, to explore how far you would
go to get what you want and why.

In many plays it's easy to determine which characters are
villainous and which are heroic. In the case of more sophisticated
and contemporary literature, the lines between good and evil are
less clearly delineated. In any case, once you're "in character," you

must never think of yourself as evil. You can't judge a role and play it, too. Leave that to the audience and concentrate instead on finding the emotional truth behind your behavior. It isn't up to you to decide whether your actions are good or bad; your job is to *justify* them from your own experience and/or imagination. Remember, characters do things for positive reasons.

Abigail Williams doesn't believe she is doing anything bad or wrong. On the contrary, she believes she can love Proctor more and better than his wife ever will. She believes she and Proctor belong together and that only she can make him truly happy. Her goal—at least in the beginning—isn't to hurt anyone else so much as it is to help herself.

TIPS FROM THE PROS

I don't much like the word "evil," mainly because it doesn't instruct. What's its opposite, "good?" Then what is "good"? Every villain is a hero in his or her own life. A few months ago I read a book about the nature of evil, and that author suggested that the opposite of evil is "hope." Makes sense to me, though I tend to favor "love."

When I took my first acting classes thirty-five years ago at New York's Academy of Dramatic Arts, I remember being taught that, no matter what, you must love your character. Frankly, I thought it was a crock at the time, but that is because I didn't know any better and was too arrogant. Time and experience have worn away my resistance and hopefully given me wisdom. I know now what it means: Begin with love. Don't begin with evil.

ED HOOKS, AUTHOR, ACTOR, DIRECTOR, TEACHER,
FROM HIS NEWSLETTER *ACTORS ARE SHAMANS*

TIPS PROS THE FROM

What does a seventeen-year-old living and thriving in the twenty-first century have in common with a young woman living in the seventeenth century? How about passion and the ability to throw caution to the wind, to abandon all and go for what she wants? In the instance of *The Crucible*, the student playing Abigail and I had a few conversations about character. We discussed Abigail's motivations; I asked her questions to provoke her to get inside Abigail, and in the process she began to align herself, her desires, and specific use of imagination with that of the character. She didn't judge Abigail; on the contrary she embraced her. During the course of rehearsal I watched the seeds of the investigation take root and by middle of the rehearsal period, the character had blossomed. The actress had really invested and personalized the situation and was able to make very specific choices that came from an organic place.

ANDI CHAPMAN, ACTRESS, DIRECTOR, ADVANCED ACTING INSTRUCTOR AT THE CONSERVATORY OF FINE ARTS, LOS ANGELES

Don't Try to Feel!

Yes, it's important to tap into your emotions in order to bring your character to life. So is good acting the ability to *feel*? Absolutely not! If you're trying to feel, you're not acting! Acting, remember, is doing! Acting is being! Feeling is part of being alive, but if you spend too much time as an actor showing us how you feel, your work will be general and mushy. Play your intentions with your objective in mind and the feelings will naturally come up in you, just as they do in life. Use yourself openly and honestly and you can't help but feel. Go after what you want. Whether you get it or you don't, you won't have to figure out how you feel. You'll know! Allow yourself to be vulnerable, to be emotionally naked, and you'll experience the right feelings, just as you shiver in the cold and perspire in the heat. Feeling isn't something you have to think about. If you can manage to stay open, to react and respond honestly, your performance will be more interesting for the audience and more interesting for you, too! You'll be surprised by what you discover about yourself and your talent.

Suppose you have a role in a long-running play. Or suppose you have to do twenty takes of one scene in a day's shoot. If you force yourself to feel a certain way, you'll run dry well before the end of the third week of performance, or well before you've gotten to take number six. If you know what you want, if you've done your homework, if you stay active and involved with your acting partner, the role will stay fresh. Different responses will come up for you each time, giving your fellow actors and director more to work with in turn.

Don't be intimidated by stage directions. Perhaps, for instance, a script indicates that an actor is crying. "He wipes the tears from his eyes." "She wipes the tears from his eyes." "She starts to cry." "He sobs." "She weeps through the next scene." In the first place, not everyone manifests emotion in exactly the same way. Second, a crying actor doesn't insure that the audience will be moved. Don't forget too, that both the writer and the director will make discoveries about ways to play scenes in the rehearsal process, and finally, if crying is actually called for, your craft will support you. There are lots of ways to muster the emotion you need. One trick you'll discover is to try *not* to cry. In most cases, it's helpful to play your opposites. If you're asked to feel, avoid the feelings and see what happens!

Preparation
Once you've done your homework, tapped into your personal well of experience and imagination, you have to make it work for you. "What do I want?" and "Why do I want it?" are always connected questions for the actor and one feeds the other. The

formula goes like this: I want (fill in the *what*) because I (fill in the *why*). Figuring out the why behind a character's actions connects its motor to your own. For example: Abigail Williams flirts with John Proctor (the action or verb to play) in order to seduce him (the want) because she's in love with him (the why).

Remember the Meisner definition, "Acting is living truthfully under the given imaginary circumstances." But suppose the circumstances are completely foreign to you, supposing the imaginary situation is one you've never been in, then what? How can you live truthfully if you haven't experienced something firsthand? In the last chapter, we discussed "substitution," coming up with an experience from your own emotional repertoire, imaginary or real, which corresponds to the circumstances in the story. For instance: You've been cast in the role of a girl like Abigail, who's in unrequited love with an older, married man. You've never been in that situation! But surely you've had a crush on someone who didn't reciprocate. Surely, you've experienced feelings of rejection and jealousy. Suppose you've never been jealous of another person's love, well, maybe you've been jealous of her talent, or intelligence, or good looks. Failing that, use your imagination, be creative! Pretend your best friend has dumped you for somebody else. Spend time on the fantasy. Remember the words "as if." When you play a role, you have to do a certain amount of **preparation**. You have to pretend down to the last detail as a way of tricking yourself into the appropriate state of mind to play a scene.

Once in a while your preparation won't be strong enough. The director will ask you to **raise the stakes**, to make a situation more important for the character and for yourself. One way to do that is to ask yourself "What will happen if I don't get what I want?" The imaginary consequences should make you feel more deeply about the events of the scene. You should be able to play your action, your objective, and your subtext that much more strongly.

TIPS FROM THE PROS

It's far less work to stay prepared throughout the day or night on a set or in a dressing room, than it is to have to start from point A every time you have a new camera set-up or another on-stage entrance. That's why I try to listen to music; it's a polite way to keep people from disturbing my preparation. It took me a long time to discover that I owed it to myself as an actor to consider the whole day on the set or the whole length of the play as relevant and important to my work and not as a time to socialize.

BOB MCCRACKEN,
DIRECTOR, ACTOR, ACTING TEACHER

Let's say you're playing Abigail Williams in her first scene with John Proctor. You've expressed your love. You've flirted, threatened, and cried. You've caressed him and clutched at him and finally begged him to pity you. But the director still asks you to raise the stakes. First, you need to go back to your initial preparation, whatever it was that helped you to understand the way Abigail feels about John. Is that fantasy compelling? Is it really the right prep? If it is, up the ante. You will never feel this way again. If you don't win him back now, you won't get another chance. The consequences as you imagine them must be unbearable, you have to play this scene as though your life depends on it, which means your preparation has to be very strong. You have to be very brave and very honest with yourself in order to imagine what it is that would cause you to fall apart in that way. From there, from that emotional place, do anything you can to save yourself. Don't decide ahead of time when or how to do it, just make sure you win him back. Fool yourself. Maybe this time the end of the play will be different! If you've played this scene for all its worth, you may feel embarrassed afterwards. Certainly, exposed. You've revealed how far you will go to get what you want. Talk about being naked and turning around slowly.

Your preparation and substitutions, your examination of the question "why," are all part of *packing* an emotional suitcase. Everything you pack has to be personal and specific. Sometimes you'll find you have to discard and rummage around for something different. If a specific substitution of circumstances or relationship doesn't stir up genuine feelings, you need to find out what does. Remember, you don't have to have experienced something to play it honestly. All the better to use your imagination. As long as you don't change the lines or the story, you're allowed to make it up!

Back to Abigail: Let's say the actress is having trouble begging Proctor for his love. What's the problem? Maybe you haven't made the back-story real enough for yourself. Maybe you need to go back and re-imagine that love affair—make it specific and clear, think about what it was like to be desired by this man. How did he look? How did that make you feel? Where did it happen? Did he touch you or didn't he? What did that do to you mentally and physically? Were you dizzy or hot or cold? Did you want to shout or whisper or hide? When you come back to play the scene, you'll be surprised how well it goes.

Much of your subtext will never see the light of day. Maybe you will never need the details you've created for yourself. Even so, they are packed and ready to use as needed. Every bit of specific and personal work you do feeds your imagination, helps you to keep your performance fresh and honest.

ACTING EXERCISE:
Making an Entrance

This exercise combines the practice of preparation with the use of the question "Why?" to create a sense of urgency from the beginning of a scene. You are going to enter an empty room to find a ring. Establish four things for yourself before you walk through the door:

1   What just happened before you entered?

2   Where do you expect to find the ring?

3   Why do you need it?

4   What will happen if you don't get it?

First try this exercise knowing exactly where you've left the ring. Then let somebody else hide it and try the exercise again.

TIPS FROM THE PROS

If the director wants more by saying "bigger," give him more but don't be fake about it. Heightened commitment means to commit even harder to what you are already doing, it means to believe what you are saying and doing . . . more. Every time a student comes in to audition I want to see how he will perform in a huge auditorium. Inevitably I will ask the students to be "bigger." Translation: more committed. The audition room is invariably smaller than the actual performance space and can alter the quality of the actor's audition. I have become fond of telling my students in rehearsal: "I have never heard someone leave the theatre saying: 'I could hear too well.'" Project to fill the space; but don't be fake and yell just for the sake of being heard.

KATE BENTON, ACTING INSTRUCTOR
HARVARD WESTLAKE MIDDLE SCHOOL, LOS ANGELES

RECOMMENDED VIEWING

Uta Hagen's Acting Class. In this DVD the late, great Hagen engages with her students in all kinds of ways. Whether she's praising, teasing, or scolding, her dedication, commitment and love of the work are evident and contagious. Available at Samuel French Bookstore.

Chapter 4

Where and When

More Detective Work

The best movies and plays and television transport the audience from one reality to another—you could wind up in a rural Southern town, a mythical kingdom, or on a different planet altogether. Maybe you'll visit the eighteenth century or maybe you'll be dropped down in the twenty-first. Many elements conspire to create the environment: sets, music, wardrobe, and props. But how does the actor contribute to this magical leap? How does your work as an artist reflect the values and peculiarities of time and place? It's up to you to ground yourself in the reality of the project. Finding out where and when an event happens and how it affects human behavior involves research and, of course, imagination.

In the first chapter, we advised that the amount of research you do should be guided by your own needs and sensibilities. Some actors need to fill in more blanks than others. But if you aren't familiar with the trappings of the period, it's your obligation to investigate. No matter how gifted and intuitive you are, you can't make assumptions without doing a bit of homework.

There are all kinds of ways to saturate yourself in a different place and time. It can be helpful to find photos or paintings from the period in question—anything visual, anything that gives you a sense of what things look like. It's also good to read firsthand accounts from diaries, journals, and editorials of the day. Pay attention to the voice and tone of the material as well as its content.

As a young actor, Mary Lou was in a production of Milan Stitt's *The Runner Stumbles.* The director brought the book *Wisconsin Death Trip*, an award-winning example of photojournalism, to the very first rehearsal. He hoped the pictures and commentary in the book, eerily reflective of the effect of the isolation caused by the weather in Wisconsin at the end of the nineteenth century, would help his actors with a sense of time and place. What better way to convey the mood and tone he envisaged than with photos that echoed his concept for the production as a whole?

Researching Time

Raynold Gideon and Bruce Evans adapted the film, *Stand By Me,* from a short novella, *The Body,* by Stephen King. It's an evocative film, a memory piece in which the narrator takes us back to the 1960s, when he was a boy of twelve. Although it takes place in Castle Rock, Oregon, a fictional town, all the other details are real.

As with most coming-of-age stories, there's a seminal event in this movie: After four boys find a dead body, their lives can never be the same. Much of the film was shot on location in Cottage Grove and Brownsville, Oregon and in Reading, California. The young actors were fortunate to be able to use their real surroundings to inform their sense of place. But how did they recreate the period—the 1960s—for themselves and for the audience?

The early 1960s, before the assassination of President Kennedy, were years of innocence and contentment in the United States. Life centered on family and community and the country had not yet been torn apart by the Vietnam War. It was a simpler time. In *Stand By Me*, director Rob Reiner, who grew up in the '50s and '60s, drew from his own boyhood to ground the story and to give it authenticity. In a commentary on the special edition DVD, he explains that he incorporated memories from his own childhood and that firsthand experience helped him to direct the young actors in the film. Familiarity with popular culture, whatever it may be, is indispensable to actors. Think how often you listen to the radio, for instance, and what our music and advertising say about the way we live now. It's invaluable in your research, if it's available, to listen to the music of the period. What do the lyrics and the melodies say about the thoughts and feelings of the people who wrote them and sang along? Is the music uplifting, or moody and contemplative? See if your local library or museums have archives that include radio broadcasts from the time, and you'll gain even more perspective about the world you've been asked to recreate. Music is particularly evocative for many of us; just as the score or soundtrack of a play or a film recalls images from the story, so can music inform your work during rehearsals and performance. It may help you to hear certain songs again and again, as it helps to go back to specific photographs, to physically remind yourself of tastes and smells that transport you to the time and place in question. These are all tools that you can use to personalize where and when and to make the circumstances of the project more immediate and real.

Rob Reiner used some of his favorite songs in *Stand By Me*: "Every Day" by Buddy Holly, Jerry Lee Lewis's "Great Balls of Fire," and, of course, "Stand By Me" by Ben E. King. The entire soundtrack from the movie pays homage to the music of the day. In addition, the actors had to be familiar with the television programs of the time like *Wagon Train* and *Dragnet* and a cartoon called *Mighty Mouse*. There are references to all of these shows in the shooting script. We're lucky to live in a time when this kind of information is at our fingertips. That was not the case when

Reiner made the film, but now, with the help of the Internet, we can find out in a few moments that *Mighty Mouse*, which first appeared in 1942, was a theatrical cartoon, created by Isadore Klein. We can discover the genesis of the character and see what he looked like to contemporary viewers. We can't help but infer that this superhero of a mouse represented a time when good easily and naturally triumphed over evil. This speaks to the relative idealism of the boys in the script and makes their loss of innocence all the more poignant.

Researching Place

It's easy to find out information about a real place. The Internet, again, gives us access to geographical locations, maps, and details about weather. If you're doing a play that takes place in a famous city, you can go to a travel agency and get brochures. Visit the travel section in your favorite bookstore or at the library, too. Use the same resources for place that you used for time. Remember, as always, to look for specific details.

What happens if your play or movie happens in a fictional locale? Figure out from the start why the writer or director has decided to make it up. Is this place pure invention, or is it, in fact, a real location with a make-believe name? How important is the locale to the story? How important is the locale to your characterization and on-screen or on-stage relationships? It stands to reason that the more you know the better, but you're the detective, after all. Use what works for you.

With where and when, as with all the elements of a full-scale production, you can only take responsibility for your own work. You can accomplish the writer's or director's vision to the best of your ability, but as an actor, you're just one piece of the puzzle. As a living, breathing person, your contribution brings the project to life. By the same token, you're a human being and not a machine. All you can do is your best.

When I was eighteen, I did a film about Jack Kerouac fans. I played a young girl who had read one of Kerouac's most convoluted books, *Visions of Cody*, and had been deeply moved by it. In reality, although the writing is beautiful, I found the book pretty much unintelligible. In one of the scenes, the director wanted me to read from the book " in the style of a Beat poet." I simply could not do it. Even after hearing tapes of Beat poetry, I couldn't reproduce the rhythms and nuances. The struggle to get this scene went on for what seemed like hours and it was truly one of the most mortifying experiences of my life. We never did get the shot and I ended up crying all alone in my trailer. I now know that it wasn't my fault and that the director was pushing for something that was just never going to happen. It has taken a while, but I now see that struggle as a positive experience. As an actor I believe you have to be willing to make a complete fool of yourself. Even though the shot was never achieved, I went all the way and did the best I could.

ROSEMARY MORGAN, ACTRESS, AGE TWENTY-ONE

Use What You Have

All that research is only a piece of your investigation. It helps to have imagined the world you're entering, but don't think you have to make up every detail all by yourself. Use anything that helps you make the leap from one reality to another, especially the elements conceived by your director and created for you by the designers and crew.

There are lots of people working on your team—from designers to costumers to make-up artists—and lots of effort goes into making the world of the production credible from all angles. In most productions, stage or screen, you won't be acting in a vacuum, unless a bare stage is in line with the director's vision of the piece. In most cases, the production designer will have constructed a set or selected a location that will instantly give you a visual and physical sense of where you are. Observe your surroundings! Get comfortable there! Allow your research and observations to settle in, to ground you in the place and time that have been recreated for the audience—and for you!

The exceptions are special effects created in post-production, such as scenes shot in front of a blue or *green screen*, or scenes that fool the audience's eye in some other way. In these instances, you won't have a visual of your environment. It will be inserted long after the actors have done their work and moved on to other projects. So if you're supposed to be hanging from the observation tower of the Empire State Building but your feet are really dangling only inches from the sound stage floor, it's your job to fill in the blanks: the wind, the height, the temperature, the feel of the steel building, and the terror of being that high off the ground. Technology is revolutionizing filmmaking every day. We can make animals talk, morph a skinny man into a fat one, and make characters disappear and appear in an instant. What remains constant for the actor is that all of this requires the use of your imagination and craft.

TIPS FROM THE PROS

I played a boy who could talk to his dog. During my scenes with the dog there was someone reading the dog lines. I had to interact with the dog as if we were really having a conversation and never look at the person reading the lines, or at the dog handlers, who were always present to give the dog signals. Sometimes it was difficult not to get any feedback from the character I was supposed to be acting with. It pretty much felt like I was acting by myself. The dog would sometimes lick me in the middle of a line, which would always get a laugh. I wonder if Rowdy (the dog) thought I was crazy always talking to him out loud?

BRANDON GILBERSTADT, ACTOR ON
NICKELODEON'S *100 DEEDS FOR EDDIE MCDOWD*

Sets and Locations

A *set* is a temporary construction built to represent a location. Some sets depict interiors—bedrooms, classrooms, living rooms, dining rooms, and offices. Other sets depict exteriors—parks, woods, beaches, mountains and jungles. A set for a play often has three walls, the invisible *fourth wall* being the one that separates the actors from the audience. It's important in the theater to learn how to use the fourth wall. Be creative! The script will give you clues, but it's up to you to dream up the details. In some plays the audience has a role to play and you'll break the fourth wall to talk to them from time to time. In most plays however, even if you get to address the audience, the fourth wall has to have a strong reality for you, a reality that may shift from scene to scene. Imagine that wall thoroughly and specifically. The more creative you are, the more detailed your imagining, the more places you have to look and use in your performance. It's another way to ground yourself in time and place and character. Perhaps you are looking out a window at a lake or a forest. Make sure you know where the trees are, where the water is, what time of day or year it is and the quality of the light. If your fourth wall represents an interior, you're the decorator! You have to know exactly what it looks like. Are there paintings on that wall? How many and what kind? Is there a mirror, or a door? A scratch in the plaster? A spider web in the corner? Is the paint peeling or newly applied and fresh? If an actor doesn't know how to use the fourth wall, if he doesn't make it real for himself, he will become self-conscious about where he can look, and limit the audience's experience of the play as well as his own.

In the theatre, while you're hard at work in rehearsal, the designer and his crew are hard at work building your set. It's unlikely, therefore, that you'll see it, much less get to act on it, until close to previews and opening night. Sometimes the designer brings in drawings or even a model to give the actors an idea of place and function. Based on those renderings, your stage manager will tape a floor plan indicating larger set pieces—like stairways and platforms, for instance—as well as openings for exits and entrances. It'll be up to you to keep those details in mind while you're rehearsing, but no doubt about it, the real thing will throw you off balance at first, even if you've been working with good substitutes for furniture and props. Once you get your bearings, though, the magic takes over. Technical rehearsals can be long and difficult, but when the paint has dried and the lights are hung, the time and place will come to life as you imagined them from the first read.

Whether for the theatre or film, a set has been created to help tell the story from a visual point of view, so look around and become familiar with the details that the designer has chosen to include. If it's an interior, how is it decorated? Is the furniture new or old and worn? How does this room fit into the floor plan of the whole building as it has been constructed, or as you imagine it to be? What do the furnishings and art say about the people who live or work in this room? The designer may have thought of something you hadn't considered, a detail that will enrich your understanding of your character and the story.

A movie set generally has four walls that can be moved in and out to accommodate camera placement. There is less to imagine, since all the sets are there at one time or another. It's the actor's job to remember what's there, even when *grips*—members of the film crew responsible for shifting sets and lights—remove an entire wall for shooting purposes. You'll notice, on a movie set, that shooting is done in a prescribed order. The first shot, which incorporates as much of set as it can, is called the *master*. *Two-shots* and *close-ups* usually follow the master. You'll shoot all the coverage from one direction and then the camera and equipment will move and you'll shoot from the opposite side. This is when you're likely to see walls coming and going to make room for camera and crew.

A *location* is an actual place rented by a production company for use in a film or television show. It's chosen for the authenticity it lends to the project. Some movies are shot entirely on location and many locations double for other places. The story may take place in New York, even though it's shot in Toronto. Since locations are actual buildings, walls don't fly in and out. A small room can sometimes become very cramped and hot when it is filled with actors, a director, the cinematographer, and the rest of the crew, and equipment. When people are confined, sometimes their moods can get a little edgy. If you experience that, remember you're trading cramped quarters for authenticity on the screen and get through it.

Although much of *Stand by Me* was filmed outside, some shots— like the evening campfire scene—were filmed inside a *sound stage* in the light of day. A sound stage is like an empty airplane hangar with no windows. It was up to the actors to create that reality for themselves, to imagine the stars above, the feel of the night air on their necks, and the sounds of the crickets and frogs.

Having done your homework, you, the actor, are expected to be able to transport yourself and the audience all by yourself, without the benefit of a genuine location. Let's say you're doing a play or movie that takes place in the middle of winter. Even if the window ledges are covered with fake snow and an apparatus above simulates a snow flurry, you've got work to do! Maybe it's eighty degrees outside! Maybe you're sweating in a parka and a wool hat with a pompom. It's your job to accurately portray the condition of being cold or hot, or wet, or humid or dry. You can use an "as if" to make the situation real for yourself. Start with what's there and imagine the rest! That's acting!

Always think of the where and when as it applies to your character. This is your point of view (*POV*). Ask yourself: What just happened before I got here? Have I ever been here before?

These questions are essential when you are shooting or rehearsing out of order.

After you've researched time and place, you have to decide how aware you are of your surroundings when you're *in character.* Your sense of where and when will be different for every scene you do, and you will decide, based on all your research, how important it is to your overall portrayal of character. Do you need to keep your voice down in a scene that takes place in the middle of the night? Do you need to raise your voice to be heard over the surf and the wind? Some characters always speak too loudly regardless of time of day. Others mumble in spite of the weather conditions. Time and place are there to inform your sense of character along with the rest of your investigation.

Your character is affected by exactly the same things that affect you in real life—relationships, temperament, generation, and culture. The more you know about all these elements, time and place included, the more authentic your performance will be!

Working Around the Clock

To be an actor, you have to be a student of the world. You're researching all the time, whether or not you're involved in a specific production. Be curious and interested in what came before and what's up next. Actors have to be culturally fluent and that starts with reading: classical and contemporary fiction; science fiction and nonfiction; history, drama and poetry; and the newspaper! As an interpretive artist, the more you read and learn about the human condition, the better your work will be. Watch the History Channel, the Food Network, and the Discovery Channel! Acquaint yourself with classic films, classical music, dance, and art! Listen to National Public Radio (NPR), stay politically aware and tuned in. Go to museums and concerts and see as many different kinds of live performance as you can! Be a people watcher and remember: the magic is in the details. Time and place have everything to do with how people feel and behave.

ACTING EXERCISE:
The Fly on the Wall

Be an observer. Go someplace you've never been before—a restaurant, a church, a department store, or a park. Notice your surroundings. Be aware of the effect of your presence in the location. Does anyone see you enter? If so, how do they react? What is the physical temperature of the place? Is it dim or bright? How many other people are there? What are they doing? After you've left, how many details about the place can you remember? Test yourself by writing them down. The more you practice, the better your recall will be.

RECOMMENDED VIEWING

Stand by Me (Special edition DVD), remarkable for Rob Reiner's insightful narration. Available through Netflix.com.

RECOMMENDED READING

The Everything Shakespeare Book by Peter Rubie, Adams Media Corporation, 2002. This is a really funny book to read and to use as a reference with any and all of Shakespeare's plays. In addtion to character information, commentary, and plot synopses, it contains background information on Elizabethan life and times.

The Last of the Mohicans (Director's Expanded Edition) starring Daniel Day Lewis. This film was shot on location in North Carolina's Smoky Mountains to represent America in colonial times. Available through Netflix.com.

Chapter 5

Auditions

All in a Day's Work

An audition is a tryout. It's a chance for the person casting the project—film, television or theatre—to choose the best actor from the pool. It's an opportunity for you to try your craft, to use all the tools we've talked about so far.

Myrl Schreibman—author, director, producer, and college professor—tells his acting students that the job begins with the audition, whether or not you get the job! Auditioning is just part of an actor's work. It's important, therefore, to take auditions seriously. Learn as much as possible about each and every one, so that you can present yourself in the best possible light. If you don't do your homework, you'll be at a disadvantage.

The Homework

The first thing you must determine is how best to prepare. Every now and then a script isn't available. In these cases, the audition is about meeting a director and talking to him for a few minutes. You might be asked on the spot to improvise a scene or to read from a working draft. It's your job to show up on time—rested, relaxed, and ready to work.

For most auditions, however, you'll be given *sides*—a selection of specific scenes from the script—well ahead of time. Whether the audition is for a school play or for a major motion picture, you're expected to prepare, to do your actor's homework.

TIPS FROM THE PROS

When I work with people preparing auditions, I expect that they have done some work on the specifics. That makes all the difference. What does your character want in the scene? Who are you talking to and what does he look like? How does he smell, talk, and move? I always encourage people to cast someone in their minds. It makes the scene more specific and it really helps when you go into an audition and you're supposed to be playing the scene with a twenty-two-year-old tattooed gang member and you're reading against a bespecta-cled forty-five-year-old casting director. What does the room look like? How big, how small? What's the temper-ature? Anything to make the scene tactile, solid, real. Ask yourself as many questions about the scene and what you want as you can imagine.

KITTY SWINK, ACTRESS, DIRECTOR, COACH

Don't worry about marking up the pages. The sides are your tools. Write on them, take out the staples, do what-ever you need to do so that, when you get up there to act, you're not distracted by the words, and you have that script as a guide for yourself.

JOEL ASHER, DIRECTOR, PRODUCER, ACTING TEACHER

For the most part, nobody in a professional setting wants to see an unprepared or *cold reading*. However, once in a while an actor will come in to read for one role and the casting director or producer will send him out of the room to prepare another role altogether. Chances are the actor did a wonderful job with the original sides, wonderful enough to inspire the room to think about him differently. Even then, nobody wants him to come back into the room without having considered the material. He's sent back out into the corridor or waiting room to prepare as best he can, to figure out who the character is and what the scene is about so that he can give a thoughtful and informed reading.

TIPS FROM THE PROS

In a cold reading there isn't time to do a long, in-depth script analysis, so you need to make a plan. Break down your sides by giving them a beginning, a middle, and an end. Whatever dramatic happens in the scene, happens at the end—so start there. Once you've identified that, look at the beginning. It starts before the event of the scene, so your character is in a different condition. Get involved with that so your acting tells the story of the scene. Next, find the climax—the turning point about two-thirds of the way through. It's where the scene stops being what it was at the beginning and starts moving to what it becomes at the end. Finally, look to see if there are any other significant moments where something happens that changes the scene. Make a slash mark or a happy face or underline—anything that will give you a visual symbol of what the moment is about. Once you've got a plan, you've got something to do. It doesn't mean that you need to follow the plan as though it is the only thing that's ever going to happen. You still want to let your intuition take over; you still want to find spontaneity. But if you've made note of the events of the scene, either mentally or right on the page, there's a much better chance that the things that you understand about the scene are really going to happen.

JOEL ASHER, DIRECTOR, PRODUCER, ACTING TEACHER

Sometimes, with school plays or community theater, it's up to you to find the materials all by yourself. If the play or musical is published, it's your responsibility to be familiar with the book. READ IT! READ ALL OF IT! If it's a musical, listen to the Broadway cast recording! Figure out which part you think best suits you, but be familiar with the other characters, too. Find out *before the audition* which scenes will be used to audition each character, especially the ones you might be able to play. If this information isn't available, use common sense! Determine which scenes feature which roles and prepare one or two before the audition. This seems like a lot of work, and it is! But think about it: Would you take a big exam without studying beforehand? Prepare for each audition just as if you were preparing to play the role.

TIPS FROM THE PROS

I teach teenagers audition and performance techniques for musical theatre. Over and over again, I'm asked, "What songs should I sing for my audition?" and "What should I do with my hands?" I choose not to answer these questions in the specific, as it stops the student from developing any personal taste or creativity. So while he/she is encouraged to listen to new, appropriate material and to find his or her own organic moves, I adhere to an equation I more or less invented to guide me and the student through all the development stages. I call it DIBS: DISCIPLINE + IMAGINATION + BRAVERY = SUCCESS! If a student develops any one of the first three, I consider both of us a success, regardless of whether he or she has little natural ability or overflows with talent!

KAREN MORROW,
AWARD-WINNING ACTRESS AND MASTER TEACHER

In a professional setting, along with a **headshot** (an 8" x 10" photograph) and a **resume** (a list of credits), every actor needs to have a repertoire of pieces he can perform in a general audition. General auditions are most often held by casting departments at regional theaters, but TV and film casting directors and agents also conduct them now and then. Most casting directors will ask actors to perform two monologues. It's best to prepare a classical and contemporary monologue and/or a comedic and dramatic one, so that you can show your range. If you're a singer, you'll want to have a couple of songs ready as well, a ballad and an up-tempo number, transposed and transcribed in the key that's best for you. Keep these performance pieces short, less than two minutes per audition piece. Casting people know within seconds whether or not they're interested and it's always better to leave them wanting more.

Chances are you'll be auditioning for musicals, too. Say you're what's known as a ***triple-threat***, a performer who acts, sings, and dances. Don't think a big voice and years of dance training alone will land you the job. These days, even with revivals of classic musicals, directors are looking for actors first. It's more important for you to be able to transport the audience with your acting ability—your way with the lyrics—than with your beautiful voice. It's not enough to sound good. Treat the songs just as you would a monologue or a scene!

ACTING EXERCISE:
How Do Others Perceive You?

We're often asked, "How will I know which part I'm right for?" Casting yourself is not always easy. This exercise will help give you a better idea how you're perceived. Get ten friends together and come up with a list of adjectives that describe the personalities of people you know. For example, cute, perky, dangerous, secretive, funny, sexy, shy...you get the idea. Write down all the words the group comes up with and make one hundred copies of the list. Give ten copies to each friend and have them write their name at the top of each of the ten sheets. Distribute the sheets with names so that each friend has one for every other person in the group. Now each friend anonymously circles the adjectives that apply to the person whose name is at the top of the sheet. Distribute the findings. You might be surprised!

The Audition Itself

We've discussed homework—preparing to play a role by establishing your objectives and defining your subtext. These are the very same tools at your disposal for each and every audition. In his book, *The Art of Auditioning*, Rob Decina writes, "Acting is a craft—one that must be studied, practiced, and developed. It is an ongoing process of learning and maturing. I believe that the actor who understands the craft is better prepared to audition than the actor who's only looking to become famous and doesn't take the craft seriously." Develop your craft; start by asking yourself the "5 W's." If you determine who you are, what you want, why you want it, where you are and when, you're already ahead of the game. Ask yourself, too, about relationship in the scene. Be specific.

Here's an example: You're auditioning for *Fiddler on the Roof* and you've been asked to prepare "Matchmaker," an up-tempo number sung by Tevye's daughters, Tzeitel, Hodel, and Chava. Assuming you've read the play, you know each sister is different. They all want to get married, but each wants a different kind of guy. If you think of the song as part of the scene and part of the dialogue—which you must!—each sister has her own objectives and a unique relationship with the other two. There's a hierarchy in any family. Is the oldest sister the bossiest? Is the youngest the most pampered? Figure it out! If you've been asked to read for one sister or another, be sure to investigate the relationships and to invest the lyric accordingly. If you haven't been told for which role you're being considered, make strong choices and let them inform your performance of the song.

If you determine who the other person is in the scene—mother, father, brother, sister, friend, teacher or stranger—if you focus your attention on that relationship, you'll forget your nerves and your reactions will be fresh and interesting, even if the person reading with you isn't much of an actor. Doing the homework pays off in an audition just as it does in performance. The actors who do best are the ones who take advantage of the opportunity to prepare specifically.

Doing your homework for a musical audition also means working with an accompanist on the songs of your choice; you'll want to consider the style of the score and the character you're auditioning for when you choose your audition numbers. If that character has a big ballad, choose an audition song that shows that you can sustain long notes and phrase a song well. If your character has to sell an **up-tempo**, that means you should choose a rhythmic, fast-paced song.

Let's go back to *Fiddler on the Roof.* You're auditioning for Hodel, whose big number in the second act is the soprano ballad, "Far From the Home I Love." It makes sense for you to choose a ballad with the equivalent emotional and musical qualities. "Distant Melody" from *Peter Pan* has the right sentiment but not the right range. "The Man I Love" from *Showboat* might work in terms of range, but it's a too much of a torch song. You select "On My Own" from *Les Miserables* or "Prideland" from *The Lion King.* When you try them with an accompanist, you fall in love with "Prideland." Your passion for this song is what will make your audition special, and hardly anyone knows the song because it's hardly ever done!

With school plays, doing your homework may mean trying the scene with a friend. It's always better to say your lines to some-body real than to play them to your reflection in the bathroom mirror and it's as important to hear the other lines spoken as it is to say your own. You may also be asked to do a monologue of your choice. Choosing and preparing the right monologues is so important that we devoted the next chapter to that alone.

Particularly for film and television, an audition is a performance. You may want to work with a coach before the audition. Why? Directors don't have a lot of time to work with actors; they want to see a performance, to know you can play the part full out before they cast you in the role. And when you get the job, especially in television, you won't have a lot of rehearsal time. Your director will be preoccupied with cameras and blocking, pre-production, post-production, and delivering a story from A to Z in the space of very little time. It's important, therefore, to make strong choices about how you want to play a character from the beginning. How do you make those choices? What if you only get sides—your scene or portion of the material—and not a whole script? What if the stage directions say you're a blonde and you're not? What if they say that you chain-smoke, carry a knife, wear a nose-ring, haven't slept in a week? How much or how little do you bring to the audition? The following audition dos and don'ts will help you with all of that.

DO:

1 Be clean, well-bathed, and have your hair out of your face.

2 Trust your preparation and enter the room smiling, friendly, and ready to work.

3 Dress to suggest the role. If you're auditioning to be a host at a black-tie event, don't wear flip-flops. If you want to be considered for the part of a tennis player, don't put on a slinky dress and stiletto heels.

4 Use your sides as a prop. If you are giving somebody a letter, reading a book, or fanning yourself with a newspaper, use the paper in your hand.

5 It's ideal to memorize your lines if you have time, but if not get as familiar with them as you can. You don't want to be *reading* from the script—you do want to have the comfort and freedom to make eye contact, to listen when you're not speaking, and to *act*. Even if you have the script memorized, hold your sides in your hands, not just because you may lose your place, but also because you don't want the director to think you're set in your ways. No matter how good your choices are, you want to be thought of as flexible and versatile.

6 Make committed choices about physical business. Decide whether you plan to sit or stand and how you plan to move.

7 If you fumble at the outset, simply ask to start again without apologizing. Ask to do the scene again if you have another choice to play. Ask any questions you have before you begin and ask, politely, when you are finished, if the director would like to see the scene performed differently.

DON'T:

1 Wear perfume. Not everybody likes it. It's distracting.

2 Prepare in the room. Nobody wants to wait while you stand in the corner with your back to the people in the room, getting yourself emotionally revved up.

3 Come in a costume. That's what wardrobe is for, once you get the job.

4 Bring elaborate props. They are unmanageable and unnecessary.

5 Perform elaborate staging. It'll distract you from your acting and the director probably has his own ideas.

6 Mime. It's not professional. You're an actor, not a circus performer.

7 Hug, kiss, or punch the casting director. If you're lucky the casting director will read well and give you eye contact but he won't want to be physically engaged.

8 Shake every hand in the room. It's awkward and time-consuming.

9 Chew gum. Unless it's specifically called for in the role, it's rude and unprofessional.

10 Make excuses for your work. No excuse is a good excuse. No amount of apologizing is going to convince anyone to give you a job.

11 Shuffle, sway, tap your feet, rattle pages, throw your pages, or overuse your hands or your eyebrows.

TIPS FROM THE PROS

Don't let the interview, the chatty part of the audition, throw you. It's okay to let the auditors know you're focused on your scene; they like to see that you're focused. Don't feel you have to pull yourself totally out of your concentration for the niceties. When you're all done, feel free to be more social.

And, for a general audition, do not pick a scene or monologue where the character is much more worldly than you are. Unless you're sure you can master that quality. These are adults watching you and an eighteen-year-old schoolgirl will look silly playing a tough hooker.

JULIA DUFFY, ACTRESS ON *DRAKE & JOSH* AND *NEWHART*

There will be times you'll be asked to audition for a role when you don't think you're right for the part, or you don't have enough time to prepare, or you're sick. Each of these is a specific case. Let's look at the first scenario:

You've been asked to audition for the role of Tzeitel in *Fiddler On The Roof* but in your heart of hearts you really want to play Hodel. What do you do? If you have representation, you might ask your agent to inquire about whether or not you may audition for the other role. In any case, do the best you can with whatever material you're asked to prepare. For all you know the role of Hodel is cast. Don't cut your nose off to spite your face with pre-conceived notions about the play or your part in it. Casting a production is a tall order with lots of elements that have to fall into place. No point in second-guessing the director or the casting director, even if you feel you are wrong for the role they have asked you to prepare.

In his book, *The Art of Auditioning*, Rob Decina writes "A first audition is an opportunity to display your potential in a role, to show how you might play that character if given the opportunity to apply your craft." Sometimes you will be asked to "make an adjustment," to do something different from what you prepared in your audition. Try it whether you agree or not. The director has already seen your choice. Maybe he's testing you to see how easily you respond to direction, to see how flexible you are, to get a feel for your sense of "play." Could be he has an entirely different idea about the character. The point is, he's giving you another chance. Try it. Have fun trying it. You may discover something wonderful! Remember, he wouldn't ask you to do it again if he didn't like something about you in the first place!

Once you're committed to an audition, convince yourself you're absolutely the best person for the job. This is your moment to play the part, after all, even if you never get to play it again. In his book, *The Audition Book*, actor/director Ed Hooks advises actors to "approach each audition as if you already have the job and are there for a rehearsal...Visualize success. Before you enter the audition room, imagine yourself winning the part. Olympic athletes use this technique all the time and you can too. See your success in your mind's eye, then go do it." Remember, too, an audition doesn't have to be and usually isn't about just one job; it's about making an impression and being considered for another part another time.

TIPS FROM THE PROS

Auditioning is a chance to act. Embrace every chance you have. It is your time in front of an audience, even if that audience is only an audience of one. It's your chance to practice and experiment. Every circumstance will be different so you have unlimited opportunities to explore. It's like skateboarding—every surface will be a different experience and the only way to master those different surfaces is to try it and feel the difference.

EDITH FIELDS, ACTRESS

Don't get sucked into annoying and dullish people who may be waiting with you to audition. Stay focused and keep your eye on the character you are playing.

KATE BENTON, ACTING INSTRUCTOR AT
HARVARD WESTLAKE MIDDLE SCHOOL, LOS ANGELES

What if you make a mistake? Is it okay to start again? If you miss a line or a beat early in a scene, absolutely, stop and start again—no fuss, no nonsense—simply excuse yourself and say you'd like to begin at the beginning. If you've nearly finished the scene, though, don't stop, don't take yourself out of character to fix it. Find your place and keep going. For the most part, producers, directors, and casting directors are compassionate people. They understand you're human. They understand you're nervous. They make mistakes too! Remind yourself they're on your side and they want you to shine. If you do well, you make their jobs that much easier!

Actors are always looking for a way to combat audition nerves. Some learn to meditate; others do vocal or breathing exercises as part of their preparation before they enter the room. What seems to work best is simple concentration. Focus. Remember your homework, the specifics of who you are and what you want, and put your attention on the other guy. If you're able to concentrate, you'll stop watching yourself and forget your nerves. Your anxiety will disappear; after all, that inner voice, the one that reminds you how nervous you are, doesn't exist in your character's reality.

TIPS FROM THE PROS

I've been auditioning a lot lately for other regional theatres. I had someone helping me with monologues and she said something that helped me almost more than anything else: LET GO OF THE NEED TO BE GOOD. It's so simple but it really works.

BOB MCCRACKEN,
DIRECTOR, ACTING TEACHER, ACTOR

We are looking for commitment, energy, and projection. We are looking for performance quality auditions. We are looking for an actor that makes the part theirs. Whatever part you choose, bring your individuality to that role.

TIM DOUGHERTY, YOUNG ACTOR

Suppose you play a scene all the way through but you feel you could have played it better or differently. It's hard for us to tell you the tone of the room, every audition is different and only you will be able to read the mood under the circumstances. We can't possibly predict whether your auditors will have the time or the inclination to hear you read again. If you're comfortable enough to ask, be certain that you really do have something different or better to play. Otherwise you're wasting everybody's time and that's what they'll remember about you!

The Callback

Sometimes, in film and television, you'll go straight to the producers for an audition. If that's the case, you could have the job that same afternoon based on that one-time read. When you're starting out it's more usual to have to do what's called a **pre-read**, an audition for the audition. You're asked to come in and read for the casting director first. She decides based on your reading whether or not she wants to bring you to the producers. That pre-read is every bit as important as the **callback**, since it determines not just whether or not you're seen later that day or the next for the role in question, but whether or not the casting director keeps your picture and resume for other projects.

TIPS FROM THE PROS

With regard to the business side of acting, treat every audition like a job interview. Be professional. This is an indication that you take yourself and your craft seriously. Regardless of whether you get the job or not, don't take it personally. You are not being judged on how good a PERSON you are. You're being judged on many factors, which vary from one audition to the next and are completely out of your control. Do the best job you can with what you have and enjoy your life, knowing that you are becoming a better person in the process.

BROOKE DENYSE, ACTRESS

If you do get a callback, for on-camera or theatrical work, you'll want to duplicate, to the best of your ability, the performance you gave the first time. Don't confuse the powers that be, particularly when you've got them on your side. If you wore a red dress the first time you read, don't come in wearing jeans and sneakers for the callback. Wear that red dress again! How would you feel if at the end of the day, long after you'd come in wearing blue, the producer turned to the casting director and asked, "What ever happened to the girl in the red dress?" Unless the casting director tells you beforehand to change your look, don't!

When it's Over, It's Over

Here's what to ask yourself once you're on your way home: Did I do my best work? And if the answer is no: Why? What, specifically, got in my way? What could I have done better? Resolve to make those changes the next time you audition and then, whether or not you did exactly what you intended to do, you must order yourself to *let it go*. That means not dwelling on something you can't control. The audition is OVER. You will or you won't get the part. No amount of obsessing or replaying it in your head will change the outcome. LET IT GO!

TIPS FROM THE PROS

An actor can succeed on all levels and still not be cast. The actor will ask, "What did I do wrong?" Usually, the actor has done nothing wrong. Put your focus on your audition. Did you do what you wanted to do? If the answer is yes, feel proud of yourself as that is all you have control of. Your job as an actor is to act. The director's job is to choose the actor he or she feels best fits the role.

KATE BENTON, ACTING INSTRUCTOR AT
HARVARD WESTLAKE MIDDLE SCHOOL, LOS ANGELES

RECOMMENDED READING

The Complete Professional Audition by Darren Cohen with Michael Perilstein, Back Stage Books, 2005. This is one of the most recent, up-to-date guides on auditioning for both musicals and plays. It is straightforward and practical.

Chapter 6

Monologues

Talking to Yourself Out Loud

So what's all the fuss about monologues? What are they exactly
and what makes one stand out from the others? A ***monologue*** is
a long speech for one character. We'll define a monologue in the
conventional way, as the great actress and teacher Uta Hagen does
in her book, *Respect For Acting*: "Only when you are talking aloud
when *alone* is it a monologue. Anything else is a dialogue!...
When a character is called on to talk to the *audience*, it is not a
mono but a *duo*logue—the audience becomes the actor's partner."

Some monologues are addressed to other characters in the
scene. Others are ***soliloquies***—that is, the character is talking
to himself. Even if that's the case, you must not forget to
communicate. Especially in the case of theatre, the audience
plays an important role and can never be taken for granted.

Monologues are most often used as an audition tool. You may
be asked to do one for an agent, a manager, or a casting director.
Many theatres hold general auditions—year round or at the
beginning of a season—and monologues are what casting people

want to see. Occasionally, you'll have to perform a monologue even if you're auditioning for specific part in a specific play. And you'll certainly be required to do one or more if you audition for the drama department of a college or a performing arts high school. Performed out of the context of the play, monologues can feel awkward and artificial. Don't let that discourage you. Find a piece of material that you absolutely love and think of your monologue as an opportunity to act all by yourself!

TIPS FROM THE PROS

As for choosing monologues to use for drama school auditions: It's very helpful if you can speak to a graduate who can guide you as to what gets their attention. Find out what they want. If they want Shakespeare, find great speeches not often done; there are plenty. Look at *The Winter's Tale* (for women), and the Henry plays (for men). Do NOT look in a monologue book! Start early. You may have to order plays from another library and wait to get them. Look at possible monologues in the play, and if they grab you, read the whole play. Have a contemporary comedic and dramatic piece, and a classical comedic and dramatic piece. Each school has slightly different requirements so you'll do best if you find four pieces you're comfortable with. Memorize them WEEKS before your auditions and work on them constantly, adding layers. Do them in front of people in both small and larger rooms. Try to keep your physical requirements minimal, maybe one or two chairs, which you can move any way you like when you get in the room. Make eye contact with the observers only if it's appropriate to the monologue... Your eyes should be in many different places as you speak, as they would be in life.

ANONYMOUS ACTOR AND MOTHER OF A COLLEGE APPLICANT

Types of Monologues

Monologues come in all shapes and sizes. They can be any length: as long as a whole play—that's a *one-person show*—or for audition purposes, as short as a minute.

There are different varieties of monologues and in the beginning you'll need a bit of a repertoire in your trunk. Casting directors will specify what sort of piece they want to hear: contemporary, classical, dramatic, or comedic. Classical plays include work by Shakespeare, the Greeks (Sophocles and Euripides), Moliere, Goldoni, Congreve, Sheridan, and Chekhov. Some twentieth century plays—by George Bernard Shaw and Eugene O'Neill, for instance—are also considered classical rather than contemporary material. Be certain you know what sort of piece is required when a casting director requests a classical monologue.

A contemporary monologue should have a modern tone and feel, relatively speaking. Contemporary may mean post-World War II, but it can include all of the twentieth century, too. For some people, anything written more than twenty-five years ago is ancient! Basically, the idea behind a contemporary monologue is that the language and the issues are current and accessible to an audience today.

As for the distinction between comedic and dramatic work, comedic means funny, or light in tone, and dramatic means serious. Even so you might find a good dramatic monologue in a comedy or the other way around. If you're asked to audition with specific material, classical or contemporary, comedic or dramatic, it's important to be sure you understand the casting person's definition of the term.

Choosing a Monologue

Finding the right material is the most important step in performing a monologue. Like your headshot, the material you choose will define you for casting people, as well as directors and producers. Choose well: Make sure the speech suits you. Make sure it expresses your individual strengths. Make sure you love it enough to do it over and over again with conviction and pleasure.

There are many collections of monologues available to young actors, which means, of course, those are the ones most commonly performed. It's best to pick material that's age and gender appropriate. Especially if you go with something tried and true, you don't want your audience to worry that your monologue isn't appropriate for you. Don't distract an agent or a casting director with a choice that doesn't make sense as far as they're concerned, even if you think you can perform it beautifully. No sense in tackling Hamlet, for instance, if you're a girl. Not for an audition, anyway. And if you can't get rid of your Southern accent, there's no reason to pick Anne Frank. Not that it isn't fine to choose something that's been done before, especially if it speaks to you in a profound way, but be sure you can play the part believably. And don't be afraid to find a piece that's new and unusual. Keep your eyes peeled and your ears tuned for new material all the time; English and history class, magazines, movies, and television can all be amazing sources. And when you find something good, make copies and file them for future use!

Finding the right classical piece might require hours of sitting in a corner in the library and rifling through play after play in search of an appropriate character with an appropriately long speech. Yes, this is time-consuming, but nobody else can or should do this work for you. Monologues are personal; only you will recognize the right piece when it comes along. Don't limit your search to plays and playwrights. Literary classics are full of interesting speeches—check out Henry James and Jane Austen. Spend some time with Faulkner and Steinbeck and Mark Twain, too. You won't be sorry.

Look in the back of this book for a list of recommended plays if you don't know where to start. They've been selected for quality, age appropriate roles, and general survey knowledge. Read a play a week! If you want to be taken seriously as an actor, you really should know who Anton Chekhov was!

With contemporary monologues, the field is wide open. Published plays are available through Samuel French or Dramatists Play Service (see appendix) and at the library, too. Actors of all ages spend countless hours at drama bookstores skimming and scanning. You'll be encouraged to browse and nobody expects you to buy everything you pick off the shelves. As with the classics, don't limit yourself to plays. So much of modern fiction is written in the first person. Look at story collections by your favorite authors; check out nonfiction, too. The shelves at your local bookstore are stocked with memoirs about coming of age, from Tobias Wolff's *This Boy's Life* to Mary Carr's *The Liar's Club.* Journalists have published collections of interviews that make terrific monologues, too. Studs Terkel's *Working* was adapted for the stage because it was full of wonderful and compelling monologues. He's a prolific oral historian, who has compiled hundreds of interviews in his many books. Barbara Ehrenreich's *Nickel and Dimed* inspired a full-length play. Look for accounts of survival and vocation in magazines and newspapers. Almost every Sunday paper includes a first-person essay chosen for its emotional and dramatic effect.

Unless you're specifically instructed to perform something from the theatre or literature, television and film are great places to find contemporary monologues, too. Let's say you hear a wonderful speech in a movie or on TV. The toughest part is figuring out how to get your hands on the words. If you live in New York City or Los Angeles, this isn't so hard. Both cities have libraries that catalogue produced scripts. The newly renovated Writers Guild

Foundation Library in Los Angeles is an invaluable resource for actors and writers. But this is not a lending library, nor may you photocopy any of the archived materials. Be prepared with pencil and paper so you can transcribe in longhand. Don't be discouraged by the idea! Writing out your speech should be one of the first steps to learning the words anyway!

If you don't live near a library with a good collection, record the targeted show or movie on television with a VCR or an audio-cassette player and transcribe the words later. We're *not* advising you to record these shows for any reason other than to lift material for your monologue. It's perfectly all right to use this kind of material for an audition but if you perform it for a paying audience, you've infringed on the author's copyright and owe royalties and/or residuals. It goes without saying (but we'll say so anyway) that distribution of pirate copies of any television show or movie is against the law.

Pick material you're passionate about. One of our students, Maggie, watched the *Gilmore Girls* religiously. She strongly identified with the character of Rory, but never knew when there might be good material for an audition monologue. She got in the habit of recording the show every week. She simply re-recorded over the same tape as she watched each episode. Finally, her tenacity paid off. One night there was a scene between Rory and her ex, Dean, in which she apologized for treating him badly. Maggie took a few of Rory's speeches and lines and pieced then together to make a dynamite two-minute monologue.

Weaving together a few short speeches is a perfectly acceptable way to build a monologue. Make sure the transitions work organically, that the material flows from one idea to the next, and feel free to add words here and there to help you. Make sure the piece has a strong beginning and end. This can be especially useful in the case of contemporary works; you'll have to be more careful when you're using material that's written in meter or verse. Never use a section that demands an answer from a scene partner and don't pretend you've heard something your audience hasn't.

John Pielmeier wrote a wonderfully compelling role for a young woman in his play *Agnes of God*. Agnes has two great monologues: Act One, Scene 4 and in Act Two, Scene 4. In both scenes, Agnes is very docile. The stage directions tell us she speaks "sweetly and sanely." Dylan, one of our students, had played the role of Agnes in high school and knew the play intimately. She recognized that Agnes's showier moments are in the dialogue scenes where the doctor is forcing Agnes to delve into her memories of her mother or when Agnes confronts her denial about murdering her illegitimate child. Dylan wanted to build her monologue around the following speech Agnes makes about her mother:

"You're trying to get me to say that she was a bad woman, and that she hated me, and she didn't want me but that is not true, because she did love me, and she was a good woman, a saint, and she *did* want me. You don't want to hear the nice parts about her—all you're interested in is sickness."

Dylan pieced together two other speeches from earlier in that same scene.

"I get headaches. Mummy did too. She'd lie in the dark with a wet cloth over her face and tell me to go away. Oh, but she wasn't stupid. Oh no, she was very smart. She knew everything. She even knew things nobody else knew."

And...

"The future. She knew what was going to happen to me, and that's why she hid me away. I didn't like school very much. And I liked being with Mummy. She'd tell me all kinds of things. She told me I would enter the convent, and I did. She even knew about this."

By adding a few transitional words and deleting some others, Dylan pieced together the following dramatic audition monologue:

"I get headaches. Mummy did too. She'd lie in the dark with a wet cloth over her face and tell me to go away. Oh, but she wasn't stupid. Oh no, she was very smart. She knew everything. She even knew things nobody else knew.(ADD) *Like* the future. She knew what was going to happen to me, and that's why she hid me away. I didn't like school very much. And I liked being with Mummy. (DELETE) *She'd tell me all kinds of things. She told me I would enter the convent, and I did. She even knew about this.* (ADD) *And* you're trying to get me to say that she was a bad woman, and that she hated me, and she didn't want me but that is not true, because she did love me, and she was a good woman, a saint, and she *did* want me. You don't want to hear the nice parts about her—all you're interested in is sickness."

Rehearsing Your Monologue

Once you've chosen your monologue, you can begin to rehearse! It's easier all round if you remind yourself your monologue is really a scene. The audience just can't see your scene partner. This is where it gets tricky. If good acting is listening and responding moment to moment, to whom do you listen and respond in a monologue? You need imagination—and craft—now more than ever!

If you are talking to somebody else in the play, which is usually the case, it's entirely up to you how your imaginary scene partner responds and how that makes you behave. Which brings us to the first line of your monologue, the most important line of all.

Before you even open your mouth, you must create the illusion that someone is playing this scene with you. We call this ***placing your partner in the room.*** It happens the moment you look up and before you begin speaking.

ACTING EXERCISE:
Placing Your Partner in the Room

This exercise requires a class situation because you need an audience. Every class member should memorize the first line of a monologue. Take turns "getting on stage," introducing yourself and your piece. "Hello. I'm Dylan Diehl. I'll be performing Agnes from *Agnes of God*…" Make eye contact with your scene partner and say your first line. Let the audience judge whether you made your scene partner come alive for them. Your audience might not know exactly to whom you're speaking at first, but if you're specific, they'll be immediately engaged and interested in finding out.

Here's what an audience should know from the first beat of a monologue: Where you have placed your scene partner and the quality of your relationship. Soon enough they'll know whether this is your father, mother, brother, teacher, or friend, but even before you say that first line, they'll have some idea how you feel about the imaginary person in the room.

Not only do you have to place that person in the room from the top of your piece, you have to keep him there! You have to continue to imagine your partner throughout the monologue. This is what will keep it alive for the audience and make it worth acting for you. All of the 5 W's apply: You have to know where you are, who you are, what you want, why you want it, and when the scene takes place. From there, decide how you're going to get what you want, and what sorts of obstacles your imaginary scene partner will put in your way. Consider the fact that nobody in the world would let you talk for a full minute or longer without reacting in some way. (Lectures are an exception but are generally too static to make good audition monologues.) Even if the other character's reaction is indifference, even and especially if she chooses to ignore what you're saying, her behavior is going to affect you! Your choices have to be strong and specific for both of you; if they aren't your work will be neither exciting nor credible, you'll just put us to sleep. Even after you've made those choices, you should aim to rediscover the piece each time you perform it, just as you would a scene with another actor.

Performing Your Monologue

When you do a monologue, place the other character in the scene within your fourth wall just above the heads of your audience so that they can see your eyes. Place them as close or as far away as the scene requires.

Don't be afraid to move around during a monologue, but don't make your movements arbitrary either. Body language says a lot about you and your blocking should be as specifically motivated as any other choice you make in the scene. If you're doing a monologue for an audition, there will often be a chair and perhaps a table provided for you. Feel free to move either or both pieces of furniture before you begin. You may have only a metal folding chair, but if you are sitting on a comfortable sofa in your scene, the audience should be able to tell by your posture. Own the space. Make sure you know what's in the room as you imagine it, and be especially specific about what's on your fourth wall.

When Dylan was auditioning with her monologue from *Agnes of God*, she knew playwright John Pielmeier wanted the play performed on "a stage free of all props, furniture and set pieces... Because it is a play of the mind, and miracles, it is a play of light and shadows." But Dylan knew that as an actress, she had to imagine the doctor's office for herself. Dylan chose to stand center stage, placing the doctor inside her fourth wall. She imagined that the doctor's office was wood-paneled and decorated with diplomas. She pictured him standing in front of his desk. This scene is Agnes's second meeting with the doctor. Her objective in the scene is to get the doctor to like her mother. Dylan uses the actions to confess, to impress, to correct, and to insist. If she can't convince the doctor she'll be forced to leave the convent, so the stakes are very high. She never had the doctor move, but she moved closer to him as her need increased.

Even if your character is addressing the audience, you should never make eye contact in an audition. Direct eye contact makes the people for whom you are auditioning uncomfortable. They may feel compelled to react, to play the scene with you rather than to evaluate your performance.

Performing a monologue in a play is something else altogether. Either you're really and truly talking to yourself (which is no easy task and requires rehearsal like everything else), or your monologue is a soliloquy and your character is addressing the audience directly (as in Shakespeare). In the case of a soliloquy, make eye contact if you can. Depending on the venue this isn't always possible. Often when the house is dark it's difficult to see individual members of the audience.

Songs are monologues too and all the same rules apply. Who are you talking to? What do you want and why? Where are you and when are you singing? Think about substitution, personalization, relationship, and intentions. Before you work with the music, write out the lyrics as a monologue. Eliminate the punctuation and try to make sense of the words as though you were speaking them, without worrying about where a phrase begins and ends musically. You'll discover clues in the lyrics, things about your character you hadn't considered, and you'll be able to incorporate those ideas even after you begin to sing in rhythm and rhyme. It's easy for a singer to fall in love with a musical phrase, to revel in the sound of her own voice in the strongest part of its range. Your enjoyment of the musical component of a song is good and necessary, but not at the expense of the words. It doesn't matter how gorgeous your tone, how effortless your sound, if you haven't bothered to personalize the lyrics; by the same token, an actor can make a song work, whether or not he's an accomplished singer.

If you're alone on stage, singing a song that reveals your character's inner feelings, consider the audience your scene partner. But again, if you're auditioning, just as with a spoken monologue, don't look directly at your auditioners. Use your fourth wall to your advantage.

Beware of using monologues that require an accent or dialect, unless you've been asked to audition for a part in a play that calls for one. Even if you do an accent very well, you'll only manage to type-cast yourself in the casting director's mind. If you're working out in class or with a coach, by all means attempt to stretch and challenge yourself. Work on all kinds of roles and particularly those that suit your physical and ethnic appearance. You'll gain experience that you just might get to use someday in a professional situation. And you'll acquire a measure of confidence in the range of your abilities.

It's difficult, with monologues, not to fall in patterns and rhythms, harder to keep the work fresh when you don't have a real live person to focus on, but if you connect with a piece of text and if you let it work for you, it's possible to stay present and to work from moment to moment just as you would in a scene. If you surprise yourself in a monologue now and then, so much the better. That's when you know you're working really well.

TIPS FROM THE PROS

Remember, a narrator has to build a relationship with the audience. Keep asking yourself, why do I need to be speaking to them? What do I need from them and why is it necessary? The answers will force you to be a better, more truthful storyteller and to create a narrator who will do much more than help the story along.

MICHELLE KRUSIEC
ACTRESS

Whole books have been written about choosing and preparing monologues for auditions. Aside from all the standard good advice, two things stand out that aren't said often enough. First, breathe. It's amazing how many people practically hold their breath when doing a monologue. Second, take time to realize every transition. Be bald-faced about it. When you are doing a scene, you can look to other characters to impel you through transitions. When you are working by yourself, the obligation is entirely yours and it better be clean and full. Which leads me back to point number one. If you're not breathing, you can't change. If you can't change, you're not making transitions. Think about how breath affects you in real life. When we become nervous or tense we short ourselves of breath. When we cry too hard, we gulp for air. When we are contemplative or pensive, we sigh. All natural transitions that our bodies make, we automatically mark with breath. Oxygen will relax you into the work and breathing will push you into a new emotional place.

KITTY SWINK, ACTRESS, DIRECTOR, PRODUCER, COACH

TIPS FROM THE PROS

Keep in mind—you must make sure that a monologue has an arc, a beginning, middle, and end—and that the character has to undergo a change. Don't just look at conventional monologues. It's possible to knit dialogue from a scene into a good coherent monologue and you may end up with something your auditors haven't heard 300 times. On that note, try to avoid monologue books. A lot of people take the easy way out. Work harder to find your material and be special.

JENNY O'HARA
ACTRESS AND DIRECTOR

I find that monolgues are difficult because you have no one to play off. In a scene, it's easier to memorize lines because you have someone to respond to, to give you emotions to feed your own. So a monologue becomes a test of my imagination!

CASEY CAPOFERRI, GRADUATE, HAMILTON ACADEMY OF MUSIC,
LOS ANGELES

RECOMMENDED READING

Plays, Players, and Playwrights by Marion Geisinger, Hart Publishing Co., 1971. This books presents a great overview of the theatre and is an invaluable reference guide from the classics all the way up to the 1970s. The book is organized by period and country, and is wonderfully illustrated.

Chapter 7

Rehearsal

How to Begin

Have you ever put together a jigsaw puzzle? That's what rehearsal is, assembling the pieces of a giant puzzle to make a picture. A lot of the pieces of this particular puzzle have to do with your research and analysis. You'll discover the other pieces as you begin to block each scene. **Blocking** is staging. It's figuring out where to enter the stage, what to do while you're there, and when and how to exit. The moment you start to walk and talk at the same time, the pieces really fall into place. Rehearsing is a matter of putting the project on its feet and practicing until you get it right.

The secret to a good rehearsal is working well and efficiently. And as with many puzzles, there are lots of different ways to approach it. Some people like to start with a corner, others work at the edges and outline the whole picture first, still others like to start with the central idea and move outward. All these methods are applicable to rehearsal. You can begin with one or try several strategies in combination, but it's up to the director to have a game plan, a definite approach to putting together the puzzle before him. Your job as an actor is to come to rehearsal focused and prepared to work according to the director's plan. Although this will be a collaborative process, although your ideas about the work should be acknowledged and considered at the very least, in the end you must be willing to adjust to the director's vision and way of working. There's a saying in the business: "There are no small parts, only small actors." Your contribution is always essential to the process and we urge you to take a serious approach regardless of the size of your role. By the same token, you must never forget, whether you're playing the lead or a supporting character, whether you have most of the lines or none of them, you're one piece of a giant puzzle.

Listening and Learning the Lines

Even within the director's vision, there are many ways to approach the rehearsal period. If you've done a lot of homework, you might want to spend your time discovering things about the other characters in the play. Veterans in the business say that the best actors are the ones who make their scene partners look good. Concentrate on the other guy. At last, having done all that investigative work, you have a chance to listen and answer. We listen all the time in real life—we have to! But you'd be surprised to discover how difficult it is when you've got a script in your hands or in your head. Many actors are so concerned about saying their own lines they forget to hear the other guy. Make *listening* one of your rehearsal goals.

Robert Anderson's *Tea and Sympathy* is a classic play with great roles for teen boys. One of our students, Charlie, played seventeen-year-old Tom, a student at a boy's boarding school in New England. Tom is in love with Laura, his house master's wife, played by Jane. Although Charlie had never met Jane, he'd done his homework. He decided to spend the first rehearsal getting to know the actress in the role, absorbing her presence in order to discover qualities about her that might be interesting and admirable. Right off the bat, Charlie noticed that Jane had a natural musical lilt to her voice. He decided that Tom loves that quality of hers, loves to hear Laura speak and laugh. The next time through the scene Charlie concentrated on Jane's physical proximity and its effect on his other senses. Does she ever get close enough to touch? Can he tell if she's wearing perfume? Can he smell her shampoo? How does Tom respond and how are his responses different from or the same as Charlie's?

In rehearsal, you have the opportunity to test your objectives and your actions. See if your plan moves you logically through the play. If it does, good for you! If it doesn't, you'll have to make adjustments. You'll have to try something different. You can't act by yourself. Maybe your choices made perfect sense when you were running the lines in your head, but how could you have accounted for the other actors in the scene? How could you have anticipated their choices? If they don't affect you, you aren't acting. Acting is about working ***moment to moment***, a phrase often used by actors to describe honest listening and answering. Every nuance, every choice, influences the one that comes next. If you pay attention, if you stay present, you'll be able to keep your work truthful and fresh. No matter how clever your choices, if you aren't using your partner in the scene, if you aren't really listening and answering moment to moment, the audience will not believe you!

In *Tea and Sympathy,* Laura remarks to Tom that she overheard him singing. She tells him, "You sang as though you knew all about the pains of love." Charlie assumed that Jane would tease him in this exchange. He'd planned to respond defensively when he said his line: "And you don't think I do?" But there wasn't a hint of derision in Jane's tone. Instead she was sympathetic and kind, almost awed by his sensitivity. Charlie had to change his reaction; no reason to defend himself, instead he had to acknowledge the compliment with the very same words.

Even while you're working in the moment, focusing on the other actors in the project, rehearsal is an opportunity for you to discover your part as it was written; you'll want to let the author's words take you on your journey through the play. Some actors learn all their lines before they rehearse. If you take this approach it's crucial to learn the lines without affect, without sense and expression, so that you don't get stuck in *line readings* (predetermined rote responses). The benefit of knowing your lines is that it allows you to focus on the acting and the blocking without the distraction of a script in your hands. You'll be thrilled at what you're able to discover about a part once you know your lines and don't have to worry about the words.

Not everybody learns lines easily in isolation but sometimes it is advised especially if there is going to be a short rehearsal period or there is a huge amount of text to be learned. If you're working on one of the classics, a play by George Bernard Shaw or William Shakespeare, for instance, the sooner you are *off-book* (lines memorized ahead of time) the better. Some classical scholars believe that with either of these playwrights and a few select others, all you have to do is show up and speak the lines with comprehension; the play will do the work for you!

Young actors often ask when they should learn their lines. If you're doing a contemporary piece, you'll be surprised how the rehearsal process facilitates memorization. If you've done your homework, if you understand the role, just showing up and saying the lines over and over in rehearsal will usually do the trick! Do beware of paraphrasing. If you resist the author's precise wording you shortchange everybody. First off, you rob yourself of the chance to discover how this character actually speaks; it's more than likely his rhythms are not exactly the same as yours. Second, your scene partner is waiting for cues; you have a responsibility to her to say the lines as written. Third, you interfere with the writer's original vision. She is the architect of the play and worthy of your respect.

Elizabethan rhetoric is the Rosetta Stone for performing Shakespeare. The true classical actor can recognize and exploit that rhetoric to transform the obscure to the meaningful. It sounds difficult at first, but teenagers are amazed at how easy it can be, and how exciting. What's more, the cause and effect inherent in the rhetoric eases the burden of having to rely on feelings for a performance. The truth is, grammar is rarely properly taught; at least, not in the way the subtleties of grammar were understood by all Renaissance school-children. Having the proper fundamentals of Aristotelian grammar and rhetoric, a young actor can amaze his audience with the power of words. Moreover, the reasoning essential to the study of rhetoric gives students specific guideposts for formulating complex thoughts and better analyzing a character's through line. The mastery of these abilities enhances an actor's joy in the spoken word and awakens his or her ability to move an audience.

ARMIN SHIMERMAN, ACTOR, DIRECTOR, TEACHER

Many actors find it difficult to learn lines until they know where they are and what they're doing in a scene. Either way, rehearsal is a process. Don't expect or even try to give a definitive performance from the first rehearsal, and don't try to duplicate your work every time you rehearse. Allow yourself to grow in a part, to absorb something different with each rehearsal and to try new things from time to time. Eventually you'll have to *freeze* aspects of your performance, but rehearsal is about discovery. Sometimes, with that jigsaw puzzle, a piece just falls into place; often it takes a while to figure out how and where it fits.

TIPS FROM THE PROS

Once you have a good sense of the script, the character and the circumstances, you're ready to learn the lines. Without looking at the script, imagine the circumstances of the beginning of your scene and say whatever you're feeling as the character. Check the script. If you were even close, go on. How far can you go before you draw a blank? Even if you're at a complete loss for words, what do you—as the character—feel like saying?

Of course you'll make mistakes and leave things out. See which lines are wrong or missing. Think about it. What's on the page is the truth; what you said may have been more right for you, but it is less right for the character as written. By investigating these mistakes you'll discover all kinds of things about the character you may never have considered. Some lines just don't stick in your head. If a line seems silly or out of character, then ask yourself: What kind of person would say that? Is there an aspect of the character that you've overlooked? In this way, you turn a mechanical job into the creative task of investigating the character through the dialogue. Don't learn your lines; learn your part.

JOEL ASHER, DIRECTOR, PRODUCER, ACTING TEACHER

The important thing for you is to find *your* way. Develop a technique of working and let it serve you without infringing on another actors method. Which brings us to:

REHEARSAL DOS AND DON'TS

DO:

1 Be on time or a few minutes early.

2 Bring a pencil and write down all your blocking. You'll be expected to remember it next time.

3 Dress in comfortable clothes that allow you to move.

4 Be familiar with the script and especially with the scenes on the day's schedule.

5 If a prop isn't supplied for you, bring an adequate substitute.

6 If props are supplied, return them to the prop table or the prop master.

7 Try anything the director suggests even if you disagree.

DON'T:

1 Don't upstage your fellow actor by standing in a position where your scene partner is forced to turn his back on the audience.

2 Be late for an entrance.

3 Talk or distract your peers when you are not in a scene.

4 Eat or drink or chew gum if it isn't called for in the scene.

ACTING EXERCISE:
Listening Exercise for Two Actors

Take a short two-character scene you've never played before. Read it through so you're clear on what it's about and decide on your objectives. Sit across from the other actor with your scripts face down on the table. Whoever has the first line should say it as written. Your partner should listen and respond truthfully and according to the author's intention. Now pick up the scripts and note any paraphrasing you may have done. Put them down and

repeat that first exchange, with the same intention but with the words as written. Continue with the next exchange, checking again for paraphrasing. Repeat the process—speaking, listening, responding, and checking the script—until you've finished the scene.

This exercise can be tedious but it serves two purposes: It forces you to listen and respond honestly from moment to moment, and it makes you aware of how your own instincts do and don't line up with the author's intentions. In this way you can determine what kinds of adjustments you need to make in order to play this character as it's been scripted.

Putting the Pieces Together

The first rehearsal of a play—and some television shows or movies—begins with a *table read*, which is a reading of the piece from beginning to end with the director or stage manager reading the stage directions. This is the first opportunity for everyone to hear the story in its entirety, to get a feel for the rhythms, relationships, and voices that are going to inform the final production. Afterwards, rehearsal will begin in earnest, but not necessarily in order. It's up to the director to decide whether he wants to block in sequence or not; maybe he wants to work on the most intimate scenes first or maybe he wants to start with the crowd scene at the end of the second act. Either way, it's his puzzle and his prerogative.

In television and film, you may not be asked to attend the initial table read. Chances are you won't see the piece as a whole until you watch it on screen weeks or months after you've finished working on it. Chances are, too, that logical sequence will have nothing to do with your own journey in the piece. In the first place, movies and television shows—except for sitcoms—which are performed live for an audience—are rarely shot in sequence. Rather, the director and producers come up with a schedule that accommodates locations and sets. If the first and the last scene of a movie happens in the living room of a house rented solely for the show, chances are you'll shoot them back to back. There's little time for rehearsal in television and film. If you're lucky, you'll get to run through your lines with your fellow actors a few times before the cameras roll. You have to do most of your rehearsal and all of your preparation by yourself and come in with a polished performance on the day you're scheduled to work. You may be asked to do take after take of a scene, but for all intents and purposes it's a one-shot deal.

TIPS FROM PROS

I'm nine and I'm making a movie, playing a total daredevil who rushes about in the quest to prove that anything already done can be done by me. One of these experiments has me plunging live wires into a fish tank, killing all the fish and suffering a major attack of conscience. So I go to the church in tattered robes and electrocuted hair to find redemption and instead end up locked in the belfry or something where I am deafened by the sound of the organist playing a new-classical piece. I go crazy. Cut to my character, now supposedly standing on the roof, fried hair and robes, conducting the symphony I hear only in my head, humming along to a classical piece that doesn't actually exist. I have no idea how to do this since I've never conducted nor am I familiar enough with classical music to hum. The director attempts to help me by saying, "Just . . . Hum! And . . . Conduct!" I end up looking a fright, waving this stick around with a safety harness strapped to my back and humming the wrong tune. I felt like such an idiot, but the scene looks good. Go figure."

SHAY ASTAR, ACTRESS ON *THIRD ROCK FROM THE SUN*

In the theater, rehearsal is your opportunity to discover how your character walks, talks, and breathes. It's about putting all those ideas in your head into practice. Don't be surprised if you feel like you're patting your head and rubbing your tummy at the same time. That's why you have rehearsal; that's why you get to do a scene multiple times. With a play, anyway, you'll have at least a few weeks of rehearsal before you perform for an audience.

ACTING EXERCISE:
Blocking Shorthand

 You'll want to come up with a form of notation to record your blocking. Ideally it should be decipherable to an understudy, replacement, or stage manager. Below is a standard list of abbreviations. Use it to describe your movement through your kitchen in order to get a drink of water, sit at your table, drink it, and then leave the room. Determine the location of the audience. This is downstage. The area furthest from the audience is upstage.

STAGE NOTATION

CS—Center stage   US—upstage   DS—downstage

R—Right   L—Left   X—Cross

CR—Center stage right   CL—Center stage left

UR—Upstage right   UL—Upstage left

DR—Downstage right   DL—downstage left

Arrow pointing down—sit   Arrow pointing up—stand

No matter how long or short the rehearsal period, use your time well. Be specific and set the bar high. Even if a part feels very close to you, don't assume you've figured it all out in the first few days. Nobody can rehearse for you; nobody can tell you how to walk or talk or wear your clothes in a role. Think how many years it's taken you to become who you are. Consider yourself: You're special and unique in every way, and so your character should be too.

I start every first session of my class with my motto: You either choose to do something or you choose not to. No excuses; excuses are boring. If a student does not prepare for class, I say, "That's fantastic! What a great opportunity for us to look at the choice of not being prepared." And when we dissect the choice we usually uncover it was fear that got in the way. It usually stems from the actor thinking he's not good enough in some capacity. To be able to talk this out in a room of supportive, nonjudgmental peers and to understand the act of self-sabotage helps the students to start making more pro-active choices not just in class but in their lives. And it's not that I am holding them accountable but rather that they are answering to themselves.

CONSTANCE TILLOTSON, ACTING TEACHER

Physicalization

If someone was to describe the way you move, what words would she choose? Are you graceful? Lumbering? Clumsy? Are you a jock? A klutz? Finding out how a person moves can be a great way into the character. If you're playing a marine, you better know how to stand at attention and salute. If you're playing a jockey, you need to know what it feels like to sit on a horse. If you're a cheerleader, you'll have to learn to do a cartwheel.

Think about your favorite actors. Maybe some of them are *character actors*, artists who play all kinds of parts and who can't be pegged or defined by one role or another. Johnny Depp, in spite of his leading man good looks, is a terrific example. He plays a rogue in *Pirates of the Carribean* and an English writer of note in *Neverland*. He transforms himself physically for each role, and not just with wardrobe and makeup.

Here again, when trying to find your way into a character physically, it's helpful to remember the phrase "as if." Always remember that as an actor you are a student of the world, a people-watcher. Friends, relatives, and strangers can inspire you when you're beginning to work on the way you walk and talk in a role. Perhaps finding an animal essence might motivate you to move in character in a certain way. Are you playing a burglar? Maybe it will help you to move like a cat. Or maybe your character is as friendly and energetic as a puppy, or as silly and playful as a monkey, or as slow-moving as a cow. You get the idea.

Wardrobe And Makeup

Don't you stand differently in high heels than you do in flip flops? Don't you feel different in a tie and jacket than you do in a T-shirt and jeans? If you're rehearsing a play, use rehearsal clothes that suggest or simulate the clothes your character would actually wear. In an historical, or ***period piece***, women will want to rehearse in long skirts and appropriate footwear—not running shoes or sandals—and men should wear appropriately restrictive jackets and pants. With situation comedy, the only kind of television where you can assume a rehearsal period, it's fine to ask the wardrobe department for permission to rehearse in costume. As long as the piece has been purchased, doesn't need altering and won't be hurt in rehearsal, the wardrobe department will be happy to let you use it.

If you're doing a contemporary piece, remember this isn't a fashion show. Loud, clunky shoes will only get in your way. Don't rehearse in sunglasses or hats unless your character wears them in the play. It's critical to get your hair out of your face where it won't distract you or the director who wants to see your face and doesn't much care about your highlights.

Voice

Maybe you've been cast because of your speaking voice and in some cases you won't have to think about it all. But voices are distinctive and memorable for many reasons, and the way you speak—whether you have an accent or a stutter, whether you're drunk or sleepy or lisping—is something else you can explore in rehearsal.

Let's go back to *Tea and Sympathy*. Tom has been drinking whiskey to fortify himself for a trip to the town prostitute. The director asks Charlie to over-enunciate his lines, something a person might do to compensate for being drunk. Additionally, since Laura will suspect Tom after only one exchange, the director advises Charlie to mispronounce one word of dialogue. Charlie chooses "permission" because it is multisyllabic, and because he can correct himself, in his effort to cover his having had too much to drink, when he says the word again in the very next sentence.

If you're required to use a dialect, the sooner you start learning it the better. You want to know it backwards and forwards, the way you know your lines, so that you don't have to think about it. Don't worry if you've never used a dialect before. There are all kinds of resources for actors, from tapes to coaches who are hired especially to teach you how to speak. As with any skill, the more you practice the better off you are. Repetition is key.

Thinking In Character

You've been rehearsing for a while now. You know who you are inside and out, how you walk, what you sound like, the quality of your relationships to the other players and hopefully, how you *think*. Next up, now that you're getting closer to actual performance, is the biggest test of all: Can you stay in character even when you're not saying your lines? Have you acquired an inner life in this role? This should happen naturally as it does with anything you learn to do well; the goal in every case is to acquire fluency. Once you've learned to play tennis, you don't have to think about the footwork. If you speak fluent Italian, you don't have to translate a menu in Rome before you order your food. It's the same with your role. Once you've done your homework, it's time to let go, to consciously play your actions and allow your subconscious to respond in character in a living, breathing way. Remember, acting is *living truthfully under the given imaginary circumstances.* Even if you don't have the next line, even if you don't say a word in a scene, you're acting!

Sometimes you'll need to check in with yourself. Have you stopped thinking in character? Are you lost in your own thoughts? Are you wondering what's for dinner, worried about your history test, thinking about that song that you're dying to download onto your iPod? Of course, if you have to ask, if you have to wonder, you've left the premises, haven't you? This happens to all actors, no matter how talented, skilled, or experienced. No point in beating yourself up about it—that's just more time away from the scene. It's listening well that will inform your rehearsals and it's listening well that will keep you open and truthful in performance. Jump back in to the moment! Make yourself listen and trust the value of all that good work. Enjoy yourself and as they say in show business, break a leg!

RECOMMENDED LISTENING

Acting With An Accent by David Alan Stern. These recordings are especially good in their specific approach to teaching dialects. You can pick up one at a time rather than buying the entire series. Available through Samuel French.

Chapter 8

Improvisation

You Do It All The Time

Improvisation is scary, isn't it? At least for some of us. Sure there are those of you who can't wait to begin, but others will think to yourselves: Who wants to improvise? I never said I wanted to improvise! I want to act! I want lines and blocking! I want somebody to tell me what to do!

But what if we told you that as an actor you're always improvising, even in performance, improvisation is part of your job! After all, no two nights in the theater and no two takes on a film set are exactly the same. Improvisation is about staying in the scene and working truthfully from moment to moment; you'll want to do that from your first rehearsal to your last performance, scripted or not, whether it's a long-running production or a one-shot deal. You'll discover that improvising is part of the game no matter what, part of why you love to act in the first place. Improvisational tools and techniques will train your creative muscles to make you a stronger, more supple, more available actor, never afraid to be in the moment, always able to revel in the thrill of *not* knowing what's going to happen next.

If you think about it, improvisation is a life skill: You do it all the time, you've been doing it since you were a little kid, you do it just about every day! Let's say its lunchtime. You're famished. You're walking down Main Street. You see a sign in the window of a diner advertising fantastic shakes and the best burgers in town. You planned to go home and have a peanut butter and jelly sandwich, but you've got a little time, so you improvise. You walk in and sit down knowing exactly what you want.

"I'll have a cheeseburger with cheddar please, and a strawberry milkshake." No improv there.

"I'm sorry," says the waiter, "but we're all out of cheddar and we only make chocolate or vanilla milkshakes." No improv there either, not really, although maybe he drops his pen or gives you a tiny apologetic smile.

Now pay attention—here comes the improv:

"Okay, just give me a regular hamburger and I'll take the chocolate…"

Or:

"Huh. Well, in that case, I'll have a tuna sandwich—no tomato— and an ice tea."

Or

You slam your fist down on the table and drop your head into your hands in despair.

Or:

You pick up your coat and slide out of the booth, nearly knocking the waiter over as you shout, "You call this a restaurant? What kind of restaurant is this? I will never, *ever*, come here again as long as I live!"

In life, of course, you don't think of this as an improvisation— although, if you indulged in that last bit of dialogue we might dub you a drama queen. The point is however you respond, you've allowed yourself to be affected by your environment and the people around you (the other characters in the scene) and you behaved accordingly, depending on your needs, desires, and temperament.

You can see, then, how useful improvisation can be for the actor. No need to be terrified, improv is for *you*! It's not a test; it's a way to get to know yourself and your character better. It's a way to get in touch with your feelings and the way you express them. It's a way to make sure you are open and in the moment, so essential to acting, whether you're performing a scene for the first or the ninety-first time! If you think of yourself as a kind of athlete, improvisation is just another exercise to keep you in fighting shape, an opportunity to discover your impulses and to learn to trust them.

What Is Improv?

If you think of the script as a safety net, and some actors do, improvisation is acting without a net. But although improv is unscripted, it is not unstructured.

Improvisation can be thought of in two ways, both of them worthy. First off, improvisation is part of your whole craft, a technique to help you to better understand a character or scene in any given script. Maybe you want to explore the moment before the scene occurs. Maybe you want to investigate an aspect of your relationship with your scene partner that isn't addressed in the story. With your knowledge of who, what, when, where, and why, you can use an improvisational exercise to deepen your under-standing of the circumstances or the relationship and to find a personal connection without using the author's words.

TIPS FROM THE PROS

Improvisation is a tool for bringing out what is unique to each individual actor. Like never before in history, today's actors are fortunate in having a huge catalogue of great performances to study on film and tape. However, to be truly original, to bring what only you can bring to your work, requires spontaneity and emotional honesty. Often improvising can help get you there.

JAMIE DONNELLY,
COACH

But improv is also a theatrical tradition unto itself with its own illustrious history and rules. There is straight improvisation and there are rehearsed "set pieces" created through improvisation. With set pieces the improvisers know their objectives and decide to incorporate elements from rehearsal in each performance. A set piece is not unlike an oral presentation in school when you have to talk for ten minutes and all you have in front of you is an index card on which you've written your three main points. Not only do you have to remember to make them, those points have to drive the whole speech, you have to get from one to the next in an organic and meaningful way. In a set piece you have an outline, too, and you know the points you need to make; what happens in between can be different each time you play, but you have to get in those pre-determined bits before the end of the improv.

Straight improvisation, or free-form improvising, is taking a premise and creating theatre from scratch. You can work out with a total stranger, provided you both know the rules. All you need to do is listen and answer, react and build on the moment before.

In *Improv Comedy* , author Andy Goldberg tells us, "The purest form of improv, the scene, is a short theatrical piece comprised of character, environment, and plot that is able to stand on its on own . . . someone being somewhere, doing something." Goldberg calls this the "premise" of the scene. He clearly explains how character, environment, and plot are the three elements of improv and how they work. There are lots of different ways to approach improvisation, but the following are some suggested rules that almost always apply.

SOME GUIDELINES FOR IMPROV

1 **Never deny.**

> If someone comes in and tells you that they're serving spaghetti in the cafeteria for lunch, don't reply, "No, they're not." As Goldberg explains in his book, "Denial momentarily stops the action. When you deny what has previously been established, everything comes to a halt while you figure out which information is correct . . . Improv is a series of adjustments. Each line builds on the previous one, and each action has a reaction."

2 **Always lay on.**

> Try adding information about the spaghetti, the cafeteria, or lunch. An improvisation should tell a story; it needs plot as well as conflict.

3 Don't plan.

Don't decide ahead of time that you can't eat lunch today because you're allergic to whatever they're serving. Discover as you go along. Remember that improv is structured. Goldberg says, "The beginning of a scene should lay out the characters and their relationship, the environment, and the basic conflict. The middle is about the characters exploring and dealing with the conflict. The end of the scene should bring it to a conclusion in some way by either resolving the conflict or concluding that the conflict can't be resolved."

4 Play an objective.

If someone comes in and tells you that they're serving spaghetti in the cafeteria for lunch, immediately have a point of view as your character. As the plot unfolds, you play an objective chosen in the moment.

5 Listen with your body.

6 Use all your senses when replying.

Can you smell lunch cooking? Have you seen it already? Have you tasted the disgusting cafeteria spaghetti before?

7 Don't try to be funny or go for a joke.

Although there are many comedy improv troupes, the secret to comedy is honesty and commitment. Take the situation seriously and let the circum-stances create the humor. Keep in mind, too, that improvisation isn't about clever dialogue. It's not about making up good lines. It's not about narrating a story and telling us your ideas. It's about truthful behavior. Goldberg tells us, "Play the role don't role play... You cannot separate good acting from good improv... Improvisational comedy is often based on exaggeration. How do you exaggerate and play it legitimately at the same time? This is achieved by establishing a character that is based in reality." You won't be funny if you try.

7 Show, don't tell.

Don't let this rule confuse you. We're not asking you to "indicate" anything. This is more about the trap that an improviser may fall into when trying to further the plot. It is far more interesting to see behavior then be told about behavior. Goldberg says, "Improvising is acting. Don't just say how you are feeling or what you're doing, act it."

TIPS FROM THE PROS

The joy of improv is that you aren't obligated to find your character's objective in the script. You create the objective on the spot. By its very nature, your objective in improv is neither right nor wrong (unless it denies), it just is. In fact, when an objective is wildly at odds with what has been set up in the scene by another actor, it often leads to a cascade of funny moments. This speaks to being funny by playing the truth... comedy is born out of making strong choices (creating an objective in the moment) and playing with passion.

CHARLES DOUGHERTY, ACTOR, IMPROV INSTRUCTOR

Every improv group has its own particular rules. Some may ask you not to touch each other. Others may ask you to refrain from mentioning body parts, bodily functions, or cursing of any kind. Remember that guidelines are just that; once you have mastered a technique, it's always interesting to push the envelope.

Situations Where You May Be Asked To Improvise

There are very specific times and places where you might be expected to improvise. This will not happen as a rule at a TV or film audition because actors' unions—the Screen Actors Guild (SAG), American Federation of Television and Radio Artists (AFTRA), and Actor's Equity Association (AEA)—will not allow it. Union members are protected from being exploited as writers or creators, by producers and directors. There are a few filmmakers, though, who always use improvisation on a set once their films are cast. British director Mike Leigh is said to use it often within a story line that he has carefully constructed. Henry Jaglom, an American director, works the same way, choosing the kind of story he wants to tell and then interviewing actors who have a specific point of view about his subject. These directors have to be very careful about casting actors who are not only perfect for the roles as conceived (perhaps, in fact, the actors inspire the roles and not the other way around), but who are highly skilled and comfortable with the language of improvisation, which can vary from project to project. You'll notice there are directors who work with the same actors over and over again, at least in part for that very reason.

Some school projects are conceived and scripted through improvisation. So you might be asked to improvise in rehearsal in order to develop the material. In school and community theatre, a teacher or director might want to use improvisation during an audition to see if you listen well, are creative, or simply work well with other actors.

Improvisation can be extremely helpful, too, when it allows you to get to know the other actors in the project. Especially if an actor is trapped in the language of the script, improv is invaluable, because it makes the objectives and the relationships clear. If you have preconceived notions about the words, or if they are difficult to say—as with the dialogue of Shakespeare or Shaw or Moliere or even some quirky modern playwrights—paraphrasing, or improvising a scene in your own words, can get you past the hurdles of verse, rhyme, unfamiliar words, or just a tricky scene that doesn't seem to make sense.

Famous Improv-ers

There have been and continue to be well-known improv companies all over the country: The Groundlings, Second City, The Wing, The Committee, Off the Wall, Funny You Should Ask, and Comedy Sportz are among them. Sometimes known as sketch comedy, these groups may look like they're playing around, but don't be fooled. The actors in these companies have spent hours and hours in rehearsal getting to know each other and honing their skills as an ensemble. The work they do together is improvisational without a doubt, but don't think for a minute it's easy.

We'd be wrong to leave out Viola Spolin, author of *Improvisation for the Theatre.* Many people consider Spolin the greatest improv guru of them all and her book has become the bible of improvisation. The late John Ritter, a brilliant improviser, in his forward to Goldberg's *Improv Comedy* refers to Spolin as "the mother of all theatre games."

There are a number of amazing shows that are based on improv. Paul Sills's *Story Theatre,* a Broadway hit in the 1970s, was created by the actors themselves, rather than by a playwright. Many *Saturday Night Live* sketches are set pieces or scripted based on improvisation. *Whose Line is it Anyway?*, another television show, features four creative, gifted improvisers.

TIPS FROM THE PROS

Imagine having a party with your best, funniest friends and you are goofing off, showing off and having the best time of your life. Everybody thinks you are really cool because you're making them laugh till they bust. It's your work but it never feels like it because work becomes play. You do this every day of your life and you get PAID FOR IT! That's the FUN of being in a comedy group.

DIZ WHITE,
CO-CREATOR OF *EL GRANDE DE COCA-COLA*

Decide For Yourself

As an actor, you are the instrument of choice—not just your body but your mind, as well. If you pursue professional training, you may or may not be asked to learn improvisational techniques. Some acting schools see improvisation as an advanced exercise, while others view it as the most basic tool. In the first case, as with other artistic disciplines, the thinking is that an artist cannot improvise until she is schooled in the fundamentals, even in classical technique. In the second instance, improv is seen as the most natural and basic way to teach actors to listen and react.

Your ability to improvise is not a barometer for your worth as an actor. While it's important to understand that all acting requires an open and flexible instrument, good listening, and truthful response, many skilled and experienced actors feel that improvisation is only worthwhile for them as it applies to the script at hand.

Improv exercises are designed to teach young actors to be specific and present. At the Neighborhood Playhouse School in New York

City, actors do improvisational exercises for a year before they ever see a scripted word. The beginning students start with an exercise called *repetition*, which allows them to be affected and to discover subtext by saying a line over and over again, until it absolutely must change.

A repetition exercise might evolve in this way:

David: You're wearing a red shirt.

Ned: I'm wearing a red shirt.

David: You're wearing a red shirt.

Ned: I'm wearing a red shirt.

David: You're wearing a red shirt.

Ned: (annoyed) I know I'm wearing a red shirt.

David: You know you're wearing a red shirt?

Ned: Yeah I know!

David: You know!

Ned: Of course I know!

David: (sarcastic) Of course you know.

Ned: Don't take that tone with me.

David: Don't take that tone with you?

Ned: Yeah, that's what I said...

And so on...

Once a student has mastered repetition, he moves on to *preparation*, an exercise that encourages him to use his imagination to propel him into a scene with a strong inner life, and an ***independent activity***, that is focusing on a physical endeavor that demands his concentrated attention. It's only a matter of time before one student is in the room busy with his activity, polishing the shoes he needs to wear in a half an hour, or writing an important letter that must go out with today's mail, when another student, full of his preparation, happy or sad or angry for specifically imagined reasons, knocks on the door. From that moment, the two actors improvise a scene.

ACTING EXERCISE:
Ying Yang

Here's an exercise taught by acting instructor, Manuel Duques, during his years at Penn State. Choose a scene partner. Decide two things ahead of time. First, what is your relationship? Secondly, what is the object you both want? The person with the object begins in the room. The person who wants the object enters the room. Each character must justify a strong need—possibly a question of life and death—for wanting this object. The exercise is finished when the character entering gets the object from the person in the room, or leaves the room knowing that the object will never be surrendered. It's helpful for the person in the
room to have an independent activity, something he or she needs to get done in a prescribed amount of time. It's better if there is a pre-determined relationship between the actors. It's also helpful to have a moderator watch the exercise to make sure it never gets out of control or dangerous. This improvisation is all about investigating strong, passionate behavior.

In some schools of improvisation, the work is not about words at all, but rather about exploring physical impulses, understanding composition, supporting and enhancing rather than imposing your will on your partners. Kate Noonan, who teaches drama at Renaissance Arts Academy in Los Angeles, uses improvisation to teach teamwork and focus. An actor herself, she's convinced young actors should learn to *do*, before they learn to *tell*. For this reason the initial work she does with her students has nothing to do with plot or story; rather it focuses on gestures and physical intentions as a way for actors to make energetic use of space and of each other. She urges her students, who may be self-conscious at first and determined to be interesting and original, to jump in and participate, not to wait for "brilliance." She reminds them that there's no such thing as a mistake in an improv; when something unexpected happens you simply have to follow through. It's her goal to get her students "out of their heads." While they're thinking, while they're making plans about what they're going to do next, they miss their moments.

The object of Noonan's exercise is to work in combinations of two and three actors. One initiates a gesture and the others follow her until the gesture evolves into something else. Her students try it out.

Deborah enters first, followed by Nan who is physically mirroring her every move. Ella enters and does the same. The girls are in sync, until Ella and Deborah accidently bump into each other.

"Uh oh," says Kate. "What are you going to do?"

Ella breaks focus, giggles, then looks at Kate and shrugs. She walks off the space in a huff.

"And what are you going to do?" Kate asks the other two girls.

"Remember, there are no mistakes, you have to use the moment, you have to follow through..."

First Deborah, then Nan follow Ella off, mirroring her sour expression and the slouch in her walk, leaving room for something else to happen in another corner of the space.

"Excellent!" says Kate.

Although Kate wants her students to work toward a goal, it's the process that's most important. She encourages her actors to be generous, not to drift and not to hide. When an improv works, when it's really exciting, everybody wants to do it all over again exactly the same way. But that's one of the most important lessons in this kind of work: For it to be truly improvisational, it has to be fresh each time. It cannot be repeated.

Find Out More

There are all kinds of books in your local bookstore about improvisation. Bookstores that specialize in TV, film, and theatre carry lots of titles as well as different manuals about theatre games for all ages. There are workshops offered, too, some of them connected with theatre companies that specialize in improvisation, usually of the comedic variety. These classes are worth investigating, as is anything that feels like fun to you, anything that makes you less self-conscious and more comfortable in your body, easier about expressing your feelings physically and verbally. Remember, as with many creative endeavors, your youth is an advantage. Improvisation is really only playing, if you think about it, and kids are generally better at play than adults. Begin now, while your imagination is supple and fresh. Keep playing, keep practicing—you'll stay limber and become even more fluent in the language of improv—as you would in any other language or discipline.

TIPS FROM THE PROS

Great acting depends on creating for the audience "the illusion of the first time." Whatever the material or the medium—from live Shakespeare to television sitcom—the audience wants to believe in the moment. They want to experience life *lived*, not merely recited. This means that *all* performance must be improvised because each moment must be totally spontaneous. Living moment to moment in performance depends on *active* listening—giving generously to your partners, accepting what they are giving to you, and allowing that human exchange to create the performance. There is no better way to develop these skills than to practice them without the crutch of a script. When you are making it up on your feet, you cannot recite because you have nothing to recite! If you try to make it on your own, you're dead. But if you listen—and play with generosity—you create the illusion for which the audience hungers. Improvise!

KEVIN T. BROWNE, PH.D.
ASSISTANT PROFESSOR OF THEATRE
UNIVERSITY OF CENTRAL ARKANSAS

What's really hard is when you come up with a great idea in rehearsal and you realize later you can't use it again, it won't be the same. But the funny thing is you always get another idea, I mean maybe they're not all great, but you know if you tried to make it work again, it wouldn't, so you just have to feel good about it and let it go."

JAKE MILLS, STUDENT ACTOR

RECOMMENDED VIEWING

The Daily Show

Saturday Night Live

The Smothers Brothers

The Carol Burnett Show

RECOMMENDED READING

Book on Acting: Improvisation Technique for the Professional Actor in Film, Theater, and Television by Stephen Book, Silman-James Press, 2002.

Chapter 9

Acting For Money

So You Want To Be A Star

Sounds glamorous, doesn't it? You've heard about gobs of money
and limousines, the red carpet, special screenings, and invitations
to exotic parties and places. Maybe you think you won't have to
go to school anymore, or that you'll wind up bigger than life on a
billboard, on the side of a bus, in an ad for toothpaste or blue
jeans or even for your very own television series.

No question, acting professionally can be lucrative and rewarding
in all kinds of ways. But ask yourself this question: Do you want
to be a movie star or do you want to be an actor? Do you want to
be on television or do you want to act? If you're not doing it
because you love acting, this is the wrong book for you. Acting for
money is fine and worthy—acting on television and in the movies
can be tremendously rewarding—but money can't be the end
goal, the reason for doing it. The truth is, show business is tough;
you're going to get knocked around, you're going to face rejection
more often than not. An acting career absolutely isn't a sure thing.
If you want to make money, consider law school instead. If you
want to make money and you're old enough to work right now,

better to take a shift or two at Starbucks. The truth is, even if you want to be an actor for all the right reasons, you still might have to get a job at Starbucks.

Professional acting is a business and as a working actor, you'll be expected to conduct yourself in a professional manner. The decision to act professionally requires a commitment from you and a commitment from your parents or guardians. There are up-front expenses and sacrifices that have to be made—this is a big investment—so take the time to figure out if you're really passionate about doing it.

TIPS FROM PROS

A child's career all depends on the parents. And the parents should be solely guided by what the child wants to do. How does a parent know when to make the effort to help her child get into the business? Is the child outgoing when meeting strangers? Has he pleaded many times for you to help him get started? Are you willing to drop everything to take him to an audition? Can you be "on set" focused just on your child's welfare? Can you afford to spend money on marketing (pictures)? Can your child focus and concentrate? How well does he take direction from you? Can you keep your spirits up when he's rejected? Can you make working a game so the child doesn't feel pressured? These are among the questions parents must ask themselves before they start on a child's career.

JUDY KERR, ACTING AND ON-SET COACH,
AUTHOR OF *ACTING IS EVERYTHING*

Breaking Into The Biz

Chances are, if you're an American actor and you stick with it, you're going to end up in New York or Los Angeles. Other cities in the country can afford you professional opportunities; there's commercial and theatrical work to be had in Seattle and Chicago, in San Francisco and Philadelphia and Austin and Boston. But for the most part the industry is based in New York and LA; New York, because it's the home of Broadway theatre and Los Angeles because it's the center for most television and film work. Both cities abound in commercial opportunities from print ads to radio to television advertising.

TIPS FROM THE PROS

When we moved to California, Will had already been in several stage productions directed by his dad. Our agent here was eager to send him out on auditions when he was five years old and we resisted. We wanted him to have an actual childhood... Not just a simulation on a sound stage. We had long talks about it with him, but he wanted to try it. So we set certain ground rules. We thought he shouldn't be a regular on a TV show until he was much older and could decide if he actually wanted to spend his life on a sound stage. We also felt he didn't have to do bad material just to pay the rent since he wasn't paying any rent. His dad and I took many TV jobs just to pay the bills, but we were grown ups—or a fair approximation. We let him audition for only the best projects. That decision has paid off: He's worked opposite Anthony Hopkins, Julie Andrews, Christopher Plummer, and George Clooney, to name a few.

NANCY LINEHAN CHARLES, ACTRESS, WRITER, DIRECTOR, AND MOTHER OF ACTOR WILL ROTHHAAR

Representation
In order to get auditions, you need to have an agent. There are agencies that specialize in young adults and others, large or medium-sized, with special children's departments. You can find an agent directory or the *Ross Report* (a performing arts resource)—both of which are regularly updated—at Samuel French and other bookstores, and the Screen Actors Guild

can give you a complete list of agents who are franchised and licensed to work for you. Don't consider working with an unlicensed agent!

TIPS FROM THE PROS

Never, never pay anyone to help your child be a star. No legitimate agent or manager charges; they make their money from getting the jobs. Your expenses are for classes, pictures, transportation, and your time. Even after you've signed with an agent, you'll be looking for projects for your child to do for free to gain experience. You'll find them on Actor Access or Now Casting. There will be a small fee to submit them for roles. Nowcasting.com charges by the month and Actor Access charges a submission fee each time or a flat fee to join Showfax.com for a year. I recommend joining Showfax so that you can download scripts for your child to read and use for rehearsal purposes. Every actor should work on cold reading-auditioning skills every day. Reading and interpreting scripts is one of the most important skills.

JUDY KERR, ACTING AND ON-SET COACH,
AUTHOR OF *ACTING IS EVERYTHING*

It's easier to get an appointment to meet an agent if you have a personal introduction. Like most businesses, the entertainment industry relies on personal contacts and referrals. If a mutual acquaintance is willing to vouch for you, it will give you more credibility. Agents can't possibly meet everybody who sends them an inquiry and a personal recommendation is one way to distinguish yourself as being serious, committed, and talented. If you don't have any contacts, a simple cover letter, typed of course, should be your first contact. Include a good snapshot and a resume (no matter how short) listing your vital statistics (height, weight, age, color of hair, color of eyes) as well as your experience and training: acting/singing/dance classes, school plays, community theatre.

You should expect to be interviewed, and to do a cold read or a monologue at your first meeting at an agency. All or none of this may be necessary, but you'll be considered professional and serious about your desire to act if you're prepared. You'll feel more confident and relaxed, too, if you're ready for anything. Dress as you do for school and try to be yourself.

TIPS FROM THE PROS

The most exciting thing about being an agent is finding undiscovered talent, pointing it in the right direction, and watching it blossom. The cool thing about working with kids is you never know where you're going to find them. They could be on the street, at a restaurant, at a friend's house, or in the office. When we see kids, we look for an energy and spark in their personalities. We're not looking for someone who can "act." We're looking for honesty. We want the real thing, not a caricature of the feelings that a young actor is trying to portray. It's important that the actor takes and follows through with direction in the course of a reading. We look for kids who possess a self-confidence that can carry them through the rejections of the business, as well as the triumphs of success on the set. Above all, we look for polite, well-rounded kids who have a passion for acting. Remember: To be an actor is to portray real life experiences, honestly and openly. It's important to have other things in your life too. You have to live your life to its fullest—passionately! When we find all this in young actors, we truly enjoy working with the elements of the business and watching them grow professionally and personally.

CAROLYN THOMPSON-GOLDSTEIN AND NICOLE JOLLEY, YOUTH AND YOUNG ADULT DEPT. AT AMSEL, EISENSTADT & FRAZIER, INC.

Agents want to see the real you, since as a child actor in film and television, you'll be playing roles very close to who you really are, or who you appear to be physically and temperamentally. Since agents work in tandem with parents and guardians, they'll be interested in meeting and getting to know them a little bit, too.

TIPS FROM THE PROS

The pressure on a young child can be too great if he feels his parents depending on him. We let Will follow his instincts with acting. He's got good instincts—most kids do. It's only an opinion, but I feel acting classes for kids destroy those instincts. Toward that end, we always let him wear what he felt comfortable wearing to an audition, even if it didn't seem to fit the character. We went over lines with him but gave him very little direction; we let him feel his way through the words and ideas. That comfort with being himself—and not what somebody else tells him to be—has paid off. He was a regular last year on a major network sitcom; he's happy and comfortable with himself. And the decision to try for a regular role was also his, in his senior year of high school. He's in an Afro-Brazilian drumming group, speaks three languages, has traveled extensively, and has a full life with tons of friends outside "the business."
NANCY LINEHAN CHARLES, ACTRESS, WRITER, DIRECTOR, AND MOTHER OF ACTOR WILL ROTHHAAR

These days, between sports and lessons and school, after-hours tutoring and enrichment, parents are chauffeurs any way you slice it; but the parents of young actors especially might as well be running a taxi service. One or the other or both of your parents will have to put their own activities and commitments on hold while they shuttle you to and from every appointment, audition, and work site. As a minor, you'll be required to have an adult accompany you to every job.

TIPS FROM THE PROS

The thing that scares me the most about working with kids in this business are bad moms. There are great, bright, shiny little kids with bad moms and I'm disturbed by the toll it must take somewhere down the line. I'm talking about the moms who just know that if they could climb into the skin of their children and go into the audition room and do the audition themselves, they would get the job; the kids are letting them down. Sometimes I'm tempted to work with one of these moms for a while because the kid is so wonderful, but I can never do enough to keep them happy. You see they also just know that if they could sit at that agent's desk and work those phones, they could make that kid a star in no time flat! Say a ten-year-old and his mom are sitting in my office, and people on the street or at the mall have told her the kid belongs in show business. She wants him to do a bunch of commercials and bank the college fund; that's not crazy, right? Okay, but they could wind up driving around LA ten hours a week for the next three years and meet with only limited success. What if you spent all that time taking regular lessons and practicing the piano? Would you prefer to spend the rest of your life able to entertain yourself and your friends jammin' on the keyboard, or able to entertain yourself and your friends with that great old story about when you did the McDonald's commercial when you were twelve?

LARRY CORSA, THE CORSA AGENCY

If an agency wants to represent you, they'll require you to sign contracts, usually for one year or for three. Your agent will receive 10% commission on every job you do under contract as her client, whether or not she actually got you the work. Many agents have checks sent to them first, deduct commission and then send you an agency check for the balance. You may be asked to provide proof that you have a ***Coogan Trust Account*** when you sign contracts. This is a bank account, named for child actor Jimmy Coogan, that ensures no one takes advantage of a minor's income under the Family Code laws. You can open your Coogan account with many banks, an entertainment credit union, and even a few brokerage houses.

Managers

In addition to agents, some actors work with managers. So maybe you're wondering about the difference between an agent and a manager and whether or not you have to have both. Here's the simple answer: You do need an agent and you don't need a manager. Many agents, especially at the smaller agencies and particularly those who are accessible and hands-on, do the same work as managers. Both agents and managers will seek opportunities for you to work. Both will submit you to casting directors and even directly to producers depending on their contacts. However, your agent is licensed to negotiate on your behalf when you get a job while a manager is not. A manager should act as a guide, should be involved in shaping your career and therefore might be less inclined to push you to take every little job. A manager may be able to open doors that an agent can't and vice versa, just by virtue of their contacts. Generally speaking, a manager will be more persistent on your behalf and more active in your career decisions. Having a manager is like having another person on your team—provided they're good players, the more people on your side, the better. If you're very inexperienced, a manager can give you a leg up. If you're in constant demand, a manager can help you juggle the offers. For those of you somewhere in between, a manager may not be necessary. The question is can you afford to pay two commissions? A manager expects a commission of 15% on top of the 10% commission you're already paying an agent. There's no rule of thumb here, no right or wrong decision, and it's worth considering that 75% of something is better than 90% of nothing—which is to say, if a manager is effective, it's worth paying out the extra money. Keep in mind, too, that your commissions are tax deductible at the end of the year.

TIPS FROM THE PROS

I have been in the entertainment business as a producer and manager for children and young adults for approximately fourteen years. I want people to know they are giving up many opportunities to do this. The mom becomes the chauffeur. She needs to know she's not the acting coach, not the manager, not the agent, but the DRIVER only. Her lifestyle, or the father's—whomever it turns out to be—will be completely different from what she or he was used to. YOU DO NOT mortgage your home to move your kid out here to "try this." Do not be in this for money reasons, and if your child is serious about acting then build a resume of good projects with good people even if the pay is deferred...I feel that a manager can develop a talent and that is what I like to do...A manager will advance career opportunities, work with a parent and make sure that this is right for the child...I always ask the children, if they're underage, *Do you want to do this or would you rather be out playing?*...If they have to think about it, I know the answer.

JUDY LANDIS, LANDIS-SIMON PRODUCTION AND
TALENT MANAGEMENT

Pictures And Resumes
Your 8" by 10" headshot with attached resume is your calling card. If you don't have them before you get an agent, you'll have to provide them soon after you sign.

This is part of that initial investment, since to get a professional picture you or your parents will have to spend some bucks. If you don't have a headshot before you sign with an agency, be sure to ask your agent's opinion before you get one. They'll be happy to steer you towards their preferred photographers and by law they're required to suggest at least three choices. Your headshot is your most essential tool, your ticket in, the only way you have to get yourself in front of producers, directors, and casting directors; it's important that both you and your agent feel good about it and it has to look like you! Don't overdo the makeup or the hair; don't try to be more beautiful or exotic than you are. Do ask your agent how to dress for the photos and be sure to include her in selecting one or more choices from your proof sheets after your session.

Once you've made a selection, you'll need to get multiple copies of the shot. There are photo duplication houses that specialize in the process. Ask your agency what they want on the front of this photo: Your name? The name of the agency? Digital submissions are increasingly common as well and it's up to you to get the required materials to your agent so that she can represent you effectively.

You'll need to update your picture only now and then, but your resume will change with every new job. Make sure your information is current. Ask your agency to provide you with its preferred format. Some agencies will ask you to put down all your vital statistics including your Social Security number so that information is easily accessible. Others simply want you to list your *credits*. It's helpful to list the company or theatre that produced each project as well as directors of note. Although television episodes have titles, you should not list the name or number of the episode and it's up to your agent to advise you as to whether or not to list the name of the role you played. Don't *pad* or enhance your resume. Tell the truth. Nobody expects you to have done more than you've done and it won't help you in the long run to raise expectations inappropriately.

ACTING FOR MONEY **123**

From the very beginning, agents and casting directors will ask to see "tape." This is not to say you should bring in your favorite home movies. Eventually, though, as you begin to win roles on television and in film, you'll accumulate scenes for your reel, and then you can create a version of your resume on VHS or DVD. Your representatives will want you to put a selection of favorite scenes together on one disk and to keep it current, just as you do with the printed version of your resume. Your disk should never be more than a few minutes long and nobody will be particularly impressed by glossy effects or packaging. Keep it simple and to the point. Present your best moments and show some range if you can, deleting the less impressive or older credits as you go along in order to keep the reel short, sweet, and current.

Work Permits

In order to work legally as a minor, you must have a work permit. The first step to getting one is filling out an application for a permit in your home state. The permit application will require a signature and seal from the school you are attending and you'll have to maintain a minimum grade requirement in order to qualify. This restriction is there to protect you. It guarantees that you will not be exploited at the expense of your education.

Applications can be picked up at the Department of Labor and have to be renewed every six months. If you register with Children in Film, in exchange for a fee, they'll remind you when you need to re-file and reapply. We highly recommend this service as well as the organization. It's a wonderful resource for and about children who act professionally. Visit their website: childreninfilm.com!

Whether you do it yourself or through Children in Film, it's vital that you always have a current work permit. Once you've booked a job, it may be too late to start this process. It's worthwhile, too, to have a current passport. Movies are shot all over the world and more and more television is produced in Canada all the time.

Education

Child actors are often the hardest working people on the set. Just because you've got a job doesn't mean you don't have to go to school. Emily Webster, now a talent agent with a baby of her own, began acting when she was two and didn't go to a "regular school" until she was thirteen.

TIPS FROM THE PROS

Child actors are little workhorses. And when they're not working, they're getting educated, going to school on the set, punching in, punching out. Sure it's show business, but it's child labor, too, not a lot of time to have much of a childhood. My older sister was in school plays, took dance lessons... Even though I was on a series, in my mind, she was the actress! I was just working! I had all the pressures of a job, I had to respond to "action" and "cut." I had to hit my marks, and in between scenes I was shuffled off to wardrobe. There was no improvisation on the set, no discussion of character or motivation. My sister was the one using her imagination and creativity. Do I miss anything about it? Well, yeah, one thing. I miss that magical time when you're reacting to someone in a scene and it's genuine and you experience that special alchemy, that moment when you don't even have to think, "I am no longer Emily, I'm completely in the moment, in character..."

EMILY WEBSTER, AGENT

Child labor laws require producers to provide an on-set teacher. In addition, the law specifies how many hours you must spend "in school" each day (three), how long you can work without a break, and the total number of hours you can work in a day (depending on your age in each case). Bring enough schoolwork to fill at least three hours plus a book to read. If you're working more than one day, the teacher may school you more than the required amount of time in order to **bank hours**. This extra time will be applied to another day when the schedule doesn't allow for enough school.

TIPS FROM THE PROS

I coached Will Estes (now twenty-six and recently on *American Dreams* and currently on the new *Reunion*) on *The New Lassie* when he was eleven and twelve. Education was important to Will's parents and they had him in a private school that cooperated with the on-set teacher, but many parents home-school their children under the same circumstances. Either way, a child actor's career doesn't always blossom into an adult career and you don't want to sacrifice his basic education. A parent has to recognize the signs when it's time for a child to get out of the business.

JUDY KERR, ACTING AND ON-SET COACH,
AUTHOR OF *ACTING IS EVERYTHING*

On most sets your studio teacher, who provides a report to bring back to your "regular school," is also your social worker and responsible for seeing that the laws are enforced. Under the circumstances, given the constraints of time and production, you'll rarely get breaks other than those required by law. It's important to understand how difficult this can be and how different from what you're used to.

Professional acting may require you to give up what you think of as a normal life. You won't have as much time to hang with your friends, play sports, or have a social life like the one you pretend to have on TV. You may have to be home-schooled. Otherwise you'll need to attend a school that's willing to accommodate an erratic work schedule and sporadic attendance. Know what you're getting into before you decide to pursue acting professionally.

TIPS FROM THE PROS

I have many children and young adults on movies, series and commercials. They cannot always be available and their lives need to be well-rounded. If they are home-schooled, for instance, and they are in high school, please allow them to go with their friends to proms and dances and to be real kids. If they cannot have the interaction of a "normal life" and I use the word normal freely, they will grow to dislike the business and only do it because of their moms or dads...If the parents are in the business for the wrong reasons, to me that's a crime. It has to come from the actor's heart and not from the moms and dads. I feel at a certain age the child should be able to make his own decisions as far as giving up an important play date or event to go to an audition.

JUDY LANDIS, LANDIS-SIMON PRODUCTION AND TALENT
MANAGEMENT

Acting as a child can be the best and the worst...My son, Jack, began acting at the age of four because he was photogenic, outgoing, and took direction well. Acting was something he did for fun, it was treated as another extracurricular. Jack never sought fame. He never wanted to be a celebrity. He only had a vague sense that money was involved. And he had a wonderful agent from a small agency who understood our priorities. We were very selective about what he even auditioned for, avoiding series television because going to a regular school and focusing on his academics was more important. Everything changed, though, after Jack played Will in the remake of *Lost in Space*. We came back from six months of filming in London and the difference in the way he was treated was astounding. He had "buzz" and everyone wanted a piece of him. The vultures moved in—overtures from large agencies and managers—but after being abroad for so long, appearing on talk shows, and traveling all over the world on press junkets, all he and we wanted was for him to get back to being a kid. Sadly, his old agent, Arletta Proch, closed shop and it's been difficult to find the same integrity she lived by. As long as you keep everything in perspective, it can be amazing. Jack benefited from his experiences by working with wonderful actors, directors, and writers. He's traveled extensively and learned about other cultures. Jack is deeply involved in another passion now—composing classical music. As a California Arts Scholar he has been mentored in composition at CalArts and will continue his studies at a very selective university in the Northeast. One of his compositions has been played on NPR after which he was interviewed without a single mention of his being an actor. He's proud of his acting but does not want to be defined by it. Chances are his new passion won't offer much financial stability so I've told him what people tell most struggling young actors: "Better keep your day job." The irony is that in his case his day job is ACTING!"

FREDDA JOHNSON, PARENT

ACTING EXERCISE:
How well do my parents know me and vice versa?

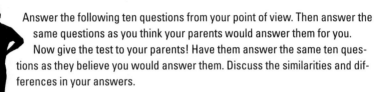

Answer the following ten questions from your point of view. Then answer the same questions as you think your parents would answer them for you.

Now give the test to your parents! Have them answer the same ten questions as they believe you would answer them. Discuss the similarities and differences in your answers.

1   Would I like to be famous?

2   Would I like to be rich?

3   Would I be willing to memorize a large Shakespearean role?

4   Would I be willing to miss a party for a job?

5   Do I care what other people think of me?

6   Am I a great reader?

7   Do I like to travel?

8   Do I consider myself a private person?

9   Do I like meeting strangers?

10   Do I love to act?

There are other alternatives to regular school. Cyber-school instructs over the Internet instead of in a school building. Most cyber-schools are public schools or charter schools governed by independent boards to which they are accountable for meeting certain standards and results. Students who enroll in cyber-schools can be anywhere in the world and still take classes. Cyber-schools offer many courses to meet the different interests and learning styles of the individual student. A student can complete his course work from wherever he is (at home, on a set, etc.) at any time of day or night; all he needs is a computer and an Internet connection. While the pace of the course work is self-directed, there is a great deal of accountability required on the part of the student. The individual lessons, homework, and chapter tests are completed online. Midterm and final exams are completed with an approved proctor (usually a certified teacher) or at the cyber-school office. The amount of time that a student spends on each course is logged and a monthly account of the time spent on each course is submitted both to the school and the state where the cyber-school has its physical facility.

TIPS FROM THE PROS

I thought I would sail through cyber-high and finish very quickly and I was wrong. The lessons are intense, and they require a long time to complete. Attending a cyber–high school takes a great deal of organization and attention to task. I've learned that effective time management skills are essential to this type of education. One needs to be extremely self-motivated to be a successful cyber-student. The computer delivers the instruction and all's well when you're able to understand the computer-based material. Frequently, though, concepts are not clear and the learning process stalls until an adult is available to break the information down for it to be understood. At times, I have found it necessary to supplement my cyber-school education with tutoring to ensure my understanding of new ideas and to reduce the frustration that occurs when I waste time re-learning or re-doing lessons. I'm grateful that I have excellent reading and writing skills, as this has been important. I do sometimes miss not being able to just walk into a teacher's office with a question and certainly I have

always loved the interactive process of learning. And
yes, this kind of education does mean you give up the
social aspects of school. Doing cyber-schoolwork in the
quiet confines of home or on a set without your friends
around to talk to between classes took some getting
used to.

RACHEL WERNER, ACTRESS

Emancipation

Emancipation is a legal term that frees a young actor from the
authority of his or her parents. It allows a minor to sign his or her
own contract. Choosing to emancipate means that you can come
to the set and work without a guardian. You are still under the
Child Labor Law Title 8 unless you complete your high school
requirements or take a proficiency test. There are pros and cons to
be considered before making this decision since it puts your
welfare entirely in your own hands. Some producers and
directors, unscrupulous or unaware, care more about getting the
show made on time and on budget than they care about you. It's
not that anyone would willfully put you in harm's way, only that
their priorities may be different from yours and this might cause
them to justify pushing the envelope with regard to your needs.
You should not emancipate unless you're savvy and responsible
enough to look after yourself in an adult, competitive world.

On the other hand, emancipation has distinct advantages for
young actors and their families. If you have your driver's license, it
may be easier for you to get to work without having to rely on one
of your parents. It's possible, too, that you will be more appealing
as an employee if you're emancipated. The production company
can work you longer hours and they don't need to have a social
worker on the set. In any case, don't make the decision to
emancipate before you're ready and do so only if the advantages
outweigh the disadvantages for you and your family.

Union And Non-Union Work

Most legitimate production companies are obligated to work
with union actors but there are companies that choose to
use non-union talent, usually for financial reasons. Complying
with union demands and rules can be expensive and union talent
is more expensive to hire than non-union, too. When you're
starting out, non-union opportunities are a fine way to get some
experience. Hopefully, your representatives won't submit or
negotiate with companies not known to them personally.
Ultimately, though, it's your responsibility and right to demand
to be treated fairly on a set, to make sure you're not taken
advantage of, and to make certain that you are appropriately
compensated for your services. You should be especially vigilant
if you choose to work in a non-union production, without a
guild to stick up for you, to protect your interests and intervene
on your behalf.

The first time you work for a union company, you're not
obligated to join a union. This is known as the *Taft Hartley law*.
With the next job, though, you'll be required to join one of the
three actors unions: The Screen Actors Guild (SAG), whose
jurisdiction covers film and most prime time television, the
Actors' Equity Association (AEA) for stage performers, or the
American Federation of Television and Radio Artists (AFTRA),
which covers most daytime, some nighttime, and all radio
employment. These unions ask for initiation fees and biannual
dues, adjustable according to your income.

There has been a history of abuse by employers of minors in the
entertainment industry. There are organizations that can guide
you through working professionally. One, A Minor
Consideration, was founded by Paul Peterson who starred as a
child on the *Donna Reed Show*.

A Minor Consideration is a non-profit, tax-deductible organization founded to give aid and support to young performers—past,
present, and future. Children in the entertainment industry are
subjected to unique pressures, and many times the images they
create outlast the money and the fame. There are consequences to
early fame, and several generations of former child stars have
joined together to reorganize the structure that surrounds the
most visible children in our society. Solid parenting can overcome
most of the difficulties faced by young performers, but a child star
must pick his parents with care. Family education is the key ingre-
dient and the members of AMC are always on call to assist parents and their professional children on a no-cost basis. By
providing a strong emphasis on education and helping to pre-
serve the money these children generate the members of AMC are
always available to help in the tricky transition issues that for
many kid stars prove to be so troubling. They've "been there,
done that." Check out what they've accomplished at
http://www.minorcon.org/tenyearstime.html.

As a series regular on a show called *Small Wonder*, Emily Webster
was recognized and teased all the way through middle school,
even after the show was canceled. She says now that "the common
plight of adolescence—the quest for acceptance—is outlandishly
compounded and complicated when one's identity is wrapped up
in a character she's played." It seemed to her that she'd never be
"normal." The effect of an acting career can be "damaging" she
explains, during those transitional years when a teenager wants so
badly to assimilate.

But Emily admits, too, that her acting career offered her a
splendid education. "Every job was a history lesson," she says, and
she remembers that her favorite role was the lead in a Disney

movie called *Caddie Woodlawn*, based on the book by Carol Ryrie Brink. "I was a precocious kid from Beverly Hills and Caddie was a total tomboy living in Wisconsin, in 1865. That was as close as I got to real acting!" Her least favorite part, was on the television series *Christy* between her sixteenth and seventeenth birthdays "That isn't a time to be doing anything but being sixteen or seventeen," she explains.

TIPS FROM THE PROS

The only advice I have is this: Don't be a child actor. It's mostly not fun, or glamorous. Everyone around you will go insane about it and either treat you like a superstar or a leper. Your friends won't know how to handle it. It will be hard to make friends. There are a lot of egos involved and yours is the last one anyone is concerned with. No one really cares about you and you will end up feeling like you are way cooler than you really are—or that you are worthless. It's hard work and long hours and you won't get to go to school dances or your friends' houses or parties or anything because you have to work. It will take over your life. Do anything and everything you can to avoid being a child actor. If you find that you love it so desperately that you can't help but go forward then you don't need my advice because you will figure it out. And to those people, good luck and I'll see you on the flip side.

SHAY ASTAR, ACTRESS ON *THIRD ROCK FROM THE SUN*

The best part of working as a child actor is the work itself; being around people who love what they do and the give and take of working in front of a live audience. The worst part is all that attention. Not that it isn't wonderful, not that I didn't enjoy it, but because people treat you with kid gloves it's hard to really grow up. In reality,

> even though people are adoring you and kissing your
> ass, maybe because of it, you can turn out to be surpris-
> ingly immature. That can affect your relationships down
> the line.
>
> DAVID FAUSTINO, ACTOR ON *MARRIED WITH CHILDREN*

Professional acting can be all kinds of fun, but you can't afford to
forget you've been hired to work. You've heard the old saying—
"There's a time and a place for everything"—it couldn't be more
apt as far as young actors are concerned. If you're lucky enough to
land a job that shoots over a long period of time, you'll develop a
natural camaraderie with the actors and the crew on the set—
actors and crew. Together, you'll become a kind of extended
family and as with all families, there will be time for play, for jokes
and conversation and confidences. But when it's time to work, all
your focus should go to the job at hand.

DOS AND DON'TS FOR PROFESSIONAL ACTING

DO:

1 Be on time.

2 Be well-rested, bathed, and have clean hair.

3 Know your lines.

4 Bring the textbooks or assignments that you need
from your regular school.

5 Bring wardrobe if you have been asked to do so.
(You'll be reimbursed if the costume department
uses your clothes.)

DON'T:

1   Don't chat anywhere close to an area where anyone is rehearsing.

2   Don't move or talk during filming unless you are acting.

3   Don't enter or exit a soundstage when a red light is flashing.

4   Don't play with props or wear a costume unless it is in the context of rehearsing.

5   Don't go anywhere without letting the assistant director know. That includes a trip to the bathroom.

Sustaining A Character

Whether you're playing a role on a long-running TV series or doing an extended run of a play, you'll be expected to sustain your character. The situations are different, but the responsibility is the same. On a TV series, the character will probably get older as you do. With a play, you're telling the same story performance after performance. Either way, you have an obligation to be consistent with the writers' vision. But how can you do that when you're growing and changing and your real life continues to move forward? In a play, you must bring the feeling of the first time to each and every performance. Really listen. Forget that you've played this part over and over. It's old news to you but it has to be new for your character every time. Notice subtle differences in the performances of others. Be attentive and specific in your responses. Putting your attention on the other guy will force you to stay in the moment.

In long-running plays and musicals, there are frequent cast changes for all kinds of reasons—name actors are contracted for shorter periods than less established performers and sometimes neither producer nor artist wishes to renew the contract. Young actors simply outgrow their roles over time.

If you're on a long-running series, relish new information about your character with each episode. Enjoy the luxury of a regular or recurring role; this is an opportunity like no other for you to relax into a part. You'll get to know more about who you are than anyone else does, but be respectful: Don't change words around without asking the writers, and don't change anything about your physical appearance without clearing it with your producers. No unauthorized transformations, please. No buzz cuts or bleach jobs or blue streaks or tattoos or piercings, however subtle, without getting the go-ahead from the people who hired you.

TIPS FROM THE PROS

Not becoming "bored in the role" or keeping your character from becoming "stale over time" can be problematic in a long-running show. Your goal is to bring a feeling of the first time to each performance. With musicals, adapting to a new cast member's vocal or dance timings, adjusting to an understudy's performance, or working with a roster of conductors gives you an opportunity to keep your character musically alive and fresh. A chance to "spark something new" within your performance every show.

KARL JURMAN, MUSICAL DIRECTOR, *THE LION KING*, BROADWAY

Guest Starring On A TV Show

Television shows are divided into two main categories: episodic and half-hour. Episodic shows usually run one hour long and you may work anywhere from one or more days depending on how many scenes you are in. Scenes are not shot in the order in which they appear in the script. Actors are usually asked to do a blocking rehearsal, wait while lighting is completed, and then filming begins. There are multiple takes and multiple set-ups depending on the camera coverage. Half-hour refers to most comedies. Some are filmed with one camera and are similar to episodic in format but not in content. Multi-camera shows will usually hire you three to five days because they rehearse like a play for a few days and then bring in cameras for the last two days of the week. Sitcoms have a very unique schedule. We highly recommend reading *The Sitcom Career Book* by Mary Lou Belli and Phil Ramuno if you have any interest in this genre.

Finally, and this goes for all actors, young and old: Save as much money as you can. No job lasts forever and you never know when the next one will come along. The Coogan Laws may require that a certain percentage be put in trust for you; even so, don't squander the balance.

TIPS FROM THE PROS

I'd never discourage someone from going after a dream. But I would tell anyone thinking about this field that there are ups and downs. You get rejected over and over again. Just try not to make it about you!
DAVID FAUSTINO, ACTOR ON *MARRIED WITH CHILDREN*

Don't get into business to make money. If you look at the statistics, you'll see they are not very promising. Have an entrepeneurial spirit and be ready to do many things to bring financial sustenance throughout your life.

BROOKE DENYSE, ACTRESS

RECOMMENDED READING

How to Be a Working Actor: The Insider's Guide to Finding Jobs in Theater, Film, and Television by Mari Lyn Henry and Lynne Rogers, Back Stage Books, 2000. A must-read for actors in New York City.

Acting Is Everything by Judy Kerr, September Publishing, 2003. Great insider details about acting in Los Angeles.

RECOMMENDED VIEWING

Inside the Actors Studio, hosted by James Lipton on the Bravo Channel, to hear professional actors discuss all aspects of craft.

Chapter 10

Acting For Fun

The Best And Only Reason

Here's the thing: if you're not *always* acting for fun, you shouldn't be acting. And by fun we don't mean giggles, romps, party time— we mean acting for its own sake, for its own rewards because it makes you feel good from the inside out, regardless of fame and fortune; acting because it fills you up, deepens and enhances your understanding of yourself and others, that's the kind of fun we're talking about.

That said, this chapter won't be a lecture about the emotional and spiritual rewards of acting. If you got this far, you know what we think, you're already there, you've got the bug, the dream, the itch and we're just here to help you figure out how to scratch it.

Many of you want to be professional actors, but you're not ready to join the work force yet, or your parents don't think it's a good idea, so you do it for fun. Some of you want to be lawyers, doctors, teachers, painters, plumbers, social workers, psychiatrists, chefs, and architects while others may have absolutely no idea what they want to be and that's fine, too. The point is, you love to act and that's the best reason in the world to get as good at acting as you can.

The wonderful thing about acting is you *can* do it for fun! And whether or not you choose to pursue a professional career, your amateur experiences in school, at camp, and in the community will inform your sense of yourself and your understanding of the world. Acting incorporates so many activities at the same time. It gives you the opportunity to become acquainted with literature and language, music and dance, history and culture and art, and all kinds of people with different kinds of sensibilities.

TIPS FROM THE PROS

Acting requires commitment: like spending time to memorize lines and attend extra rehearsals. But for me it's not a sacrifice, it's what I love. To prepare for an audition, I choose a monologue from a show that's the same type of show as the one I'm auditioning for and memorize it, performing for other people as well, to get some feedback. If it's a musical audition, I research the musical a little bit, then choose a song from another musical that may remind the director of the role I want and make him think I could play that part. It's a good idea to know what part you are trying to get ahead of time, so you can go for it all the way in the audition.

KATIE FIELDS, SENIOR AT WELLESLEY HIGH SCHOOL

Acting is all about putting yourself in somebody else's shoes. It's a lesson in tolerance. It's a way to get your mind off yourself and your problems. It's physically and intellectually challenging. And although acting professionally as a kid requires sacrifices, and impacts your family and school life in ways that might cause you to grow up too fast, or too slowly, or not at all, acting for fun is an entirely different kind of occupation. It demands focus and commitment, of course, as any of your activities do—sports, music, art, community service, religious study—but like all those other pursuits, it's not going to take you away from your regular life, it's going to support your normal growth and development. You'll meet new people, make new friends, learn new skills, and find that what you do as an amateur actor influences other parts of your life in surprising and wonderful ways. Stretching in this direction opens you up for all kinds of other experiences, exercises your imagination and your creativity, and builds confidence, too.

The authors are living proof that acting can serve you in other professions. Mary Lou has found that her firsthand knowledge of acting is the single best resource she has as a director while Dinah's discovered that the urge to act and to write come from a similar creative impulse and that both require the same vulnerability, deep focus, and attention to detail.

It's to your benefit to take acting for fun seriously. Don't think it isn't every bit as important as acting for money. It's just that it's up to you to make and follow through with your commitment to the project. Your parents might be minimally involved, as they are in your other in school and after-school pursuits, but acting for fun doesn't require any more sacrifice or investment on their part than it does to get you to soccer practice. You don't need agents or managers to act for fun. You don't need headshots or a resume and nobody's going to ask you for tape. Still, you have to be fully committed and respectful of the people with whom you're working. You have to want to act as conscientiously as if you had signed a contract and were being paid. You have to make it a priority. Even if you're acting for fun, you have to behave like a pro.

Acting In School
Most schools, starting in the elementary grades, will offer you the opportunity to participate in some sort of performance or play. Sometimes the school play is an original production, conceived and written by the teachers or even the students themselves. Especially in middle and high school, you'll have

more than one chance to act during the school year. There's often a winter production and a spring production and one of them is usually a musical. Certainly, once you're in college, depending on the school, there can be significantly more opportunities. At Yale University, for instance, each college (or dorm) has its own dramat, or drama club. There are plenty of opportunites to audition given the fact that there are twelve of these dorms and that each stages a couple of plays a year (directed and produced by the students themselves); that's at least twenty-four productions. There are also opportunities at the Yale Dramat, an extracurricular organization which serves the entire undergraduate population and produces relatively big-budget projects in conjunction with professional directing talent from New York or Boston, or from the Yale Drama School itself.

Other universities have drama clubs, too. Penn State has the Thespians which is one of the oldest clubs in the nation. It was founded in 1897 and has been continually running ever since. Any student can audition for any show, no matter her major.

Auditioning for a school play is not so different from auditioning for any other production. You'll want to familiarize yourself with the project ahead of time. Probably you'll be reading from the script or singing from the score, but your preparation is the same: You need to ask yourself the 5 W's and get as comfortable as possible with the material. You'll come in just as you would for any audition—ready to work with no excuses or apologies and having made strong choices about the scenes you've prepared. In most cases with school plays, you'll audition for the role of your choice. This means you have to know yourself well, your strengths and your weaknesses, and you have to have a good idea of how you are perceived in the world.

Especially in student productions, at school and at summer camp, actors play roles for which they're not perfectly suited. Say you're in high school and nobody's over eighteen. Somebody still has to play the mother, the father, the old man, the old woman, the teachers, the doctors, and even the narrators, in some cases. Even in school productions, casting needs to make sense. The *ingénue* or *juvenile lead* usually goes to the actor who looks right for the role. If you don't look like the girl or boy next door you might get to play Annie Sullivan or Don Quixote, Mother Courage or Tevye, regardless of your height, sex, age, or the color of your hair. Think of these as opportunities to do things you might never get to do in the professional world. Be brave! Your courage will serve you in ways you can't possibly imagine!

For Sitcom Camp, a summer program developed by US Performing Arts at the School for Theatre, Film and Television at the University of California at Los Angeles (UCLA), Mary Lou's students auditioned for three scenes from *That 70's Show*. Every boy wanted to play Kelso, the Ashton Kutcher role. Nobody wanted to audition for the role of the father, Red. Eventually Josh, a promising young actor, was cast in the part. Turned out he was up to the challenge and loved playing a character older and different from himself. His role turned out to be one of the most satisfying—and one of the biggest, too!

There's no reason that a girl can't be convincing in the role of a boy. If you haven't seen HBO's *Angels in America*, it's worth watching just for Meryl Streep's performance. Streep is blonde, middle-aged, a mother of four, and a two-time Academy Award–winner, and she plays an ancient little rabbi from Brooklyn in the television version of the Tony Kushner's Tony Award–winning play. Jeffrey Mays has received multiple awards, including a Tony, for playing thirty different roles in the Pulitzer Prize–winning play, *I Am My Own Wife*. Women play all the roles for Los Angeles Women's Shakespeare, a renowned, professional company in Southern California. These sorts of transformations rarely happen in television and film, but they're part of the magic of the theatre. Don't feel slighted if you're cast in a role you feel doesn't perfectly suit you. Dig in and learn from the experience. Do the best job you can. Discover and cultivate your talent and your craft. Character acting is tremendously challenging, perhaps the most rewarding work of all, and for some of you, your best opportunities will come to you in school where the casting pool is limited to people under eighteen. Not everybody in the senior class can play George or Emily in *Our Town*. Not every boy can play Peter in *The Diary of Anne Frank*. Somebody has to be Anne's father, Mr. Frank. Not every girl can be Maria in *The Sound of Music*. Somebody has to play Mother Superior. Embrace the opportunity to play supporting roles and know you'll be a better actor for having given those parts your very best effort.

Below is a list of Dinah's favorite roles, all played before she was twenty-three.

At Waukeela Camp For Girls:
- Billy in *Carousel* (male, a rogue, in love with Julie Jordan!)
- The King in *The King and I* (male, a King!, Siamese)
- The Captain in *The Sound of Music* (male and a father of teenage kids!)

At Pelham Memorial High School:
- Mame in *Auntie Mame* (female, indeterminate age, but somebody's aunt, and Dinah was only fourteen)
- Joanne in *Company* (female, 40–50 years old, as tough as they come)

At the Yale Dramat (in her senior year as an American Studies major at Yale College):
- Momma Rose in *Gypsy* (40–50 years old)

At the Weathervane Theatre Company in Whitefield, New Hampshire :
- Bloody Mary in *South Pacific* (middle-aged, Polynesian)

- Helga Ten Dorp in *Deathtrap* (middle-aged, Scandinavian)

Off-Off Broadway:
- Holofernes in *Love's Labors Lost* (written for a man of indeterminate age)

ACTING EXERCISE:
Make a Wish List

Write down the dream list of the roles you'd like to play. Choose from films, television, plays, and musicals. Be creative. Don't let age, gender, or race limit your wishing. Try to come up with at least ten roles.

Performing Arts Training

In most cities, public education offers alternatives geared to kids who are interested in the arts starting in high school. New York has a high school of the performing arts. Los Angeles has Los Angeles County School of the Arts (LACSA), and Hamilton High School which is famous for its programs in music and musical theatre. You'll have to audition to get into these specialized programs and once accepted you'll have to fulfill your regular academic requirements alongside your enriched curriculum. Some public schools and most private schools offer an array of classes in the performing arts, not just after-school clubs but electives for academic credit.

We asked Rob Duval, an acting teacher in Los Angeles, to share his thoughts on the value of a performing arts education He was reminded of a quote from Jane Alexander, the former head of the National Endowment for the Arts: "When we teach a child to sing or play an instrument, we teach her to listen. When we teach a child to draw, we teach him to see. When we teach a child to dance, we teach him about body and about space. When we teach a child design, we teach her the geometry of the world."

TIPS FROM THE PROS

As a high school theatre instructor, the past seven years of my life have been incredibly gratifying. Through the medium of theatre, I strive to effectively impart what I call the "four Cs": communication, collaboration, cooperation, and confidence. These skills benefit students well beyond the stage and the classroom. They are skills for life. I have seen shy thirteen-year-old students become courageous eighteen-year-old adults. I have worked with socially ostracized students who have later been elected presidents of their class. I have been privileged to witness the maturation process and know that theatre has played a major role in that continuum. Looking back at these success stories and others, theatre courses and theatre productions have positively changed students' lives.

ROB DUVAL, THEATRE INSTRUCTOR AT THE WINDWARD SCHOOL, AND VISITING ASSISTANT PROFESSOR AT UCLA

If you're truly serious about acting, if you're considering a career in the performing arts—and even if you're not—you may want to continue to specialize in college. On the other hand, you may choose to complete your bachelor's degree in liberal arts or science before applying to professional schools, where, depending on the program, you can earn a Certificate of Acting or a Masters of Fine Arts in Theatre. Most of these schools require an audition for acceptance into the program.

TIPS FROM THE PROS

As tricky as it is to schedule an audition for a college program, try your best to schedule the schools you're *least* interested in first. As the process becomes familiar you'll loosen up considerably. I eavesdropped on all of my daughters's auditions. The first two she did were the only two schools where she wasn't accepted. The difference between the earlier and later auditions was huge. Second, audition for as many schools as possible. They make choices based on their own peculiar attitudes. One may love you, one may hate you, it's so subjective. And be sure to constantly monitor your application process. Schools fill the audition slots early and if you don't get a slot you can't audition. Make phone calls, be proactive, be sure you know what's happening with your application and audition request at all times.

ANONYMOUS MOTHER OF COLLEGE APPLICANT

There are wonderful graduate and professional programs all over the country but the application process is competitive and requires research, preparation, commitment, and strength of character. The audition process may mean traveling to different cities and encountering some less than welcoming situations.

A smaller program might suit you better. There may be more opportunities in a less competitive atmosphere that may be better conducive to learning, growth, and exploration.

TIPS FROM THE PROS

There were two women at two different schools who were hostile toward my daughter from the moment she walked in the room. I remember thinking I should have told her not to look so made-up and pretty. It took me a while to put my finger on it, but basically everyone has their biases, and sometimes there's a built-in resentment toward the pretty, ingenue types, the ones who will probably get cast in the long-run based on those personal qualities. The directors of the programs made a point of telling us, ad nauseum, that the kids would be expected to hang lights for the first two years. I realized my daughter—as she was presenting herself at that time—was not what they valued. There can be a certain arrogance in academic theatre programs and I think the prospective student needs to take pains to present herself as a serious actor.

ANONYMOUS MOTHER OF COLLEGE APPLICANT

Overall, I found the audition process grueling. There were so many kids auditioning for so few spots. It's like trying to break into major league baseball. Since I knew the odds were slim going in I had Kelly audition for thirteen schools. Some of the schools didn't make much of an effort to put the kids at ease. Others did. During a few of the auditions, Kelly was actually directed to perform her prepared monologues in more than one way. Kelly was accepted academically to seven schools. But in spite of positive feedback from a number of them, she was only acccepted by the College of Santa Fe for musical theatre. And they were very selective; they auditioned hundreds of kids and only took fifteen for theatre and musical theatre combined. We went to visit and were pleasantly surprised. It's a small liberal arts school, but three-fourths of the students are film/TV,

documentary, theatre, and art majors. The faculty has
impressive credentials. The film department is state of
the art and the theatre facilities are great, too. They do
four shows a year, six performances of each, and
freshman can audition which isn't true at lots of other
schools. The theatre students act in the film students'
productions, too. The campus has a very artsy feel to it
and Kelly immediately felt at home. I think she'll really
thrive there. She's already talking about starting a
comedy improv team and spearheading some student-
produced shows.

KELLY MARTENEY'S MOTHER

Summer Camp And Community Theatre

If the school play isn't enough for you, there are loads of
opportunities to act for fun in after-school enrichment programs,
at camps all over the country, and even in the community. The
authors, Mary Lou and Dinah, have both taught at US Performing
Arts camps (www.usperformingartscamps.com). They like the
idea that students can explore one or many disciplines over a
summer stay.

What's expected of you if you participate in an after-school
drama program? Sometimes it's just a matter of showing up to a
class, the way you show up for baseball practice or karate or
music or art lessons. But eventually, as with any activity, you'll be
asked to do more, to think about what's happening in class even
when you're not there. Which is to say you'll have homework. In
the case of acting classes, your homework might involve nothing
more than being more mindful in your daily activities. You may
be asked to keep a journal, to observe people more closely, to
recreate private moments in your daily life for an exercise in class.
As you become more advanced, perhaps you'll be assigned a
partner and a scene to rehearse on your own time. You'll be

expected to break down the scene, to memorize your lines, and to provide appropriate wardrobe and props as well.

TIPS FROM PROS THE

I believe artists evolve through the excellence of their craft and the depth of their passion. The myth that perpetuates the "15 minutes of fame" syndrome is one that I'd like to see dispelled. Great actors have many voices, starting in youth and developing richly over the years, and students need to increase their arsenal of artistic tools through continued study. Building a craft takes a lifetime. It's about "process" and it's important to learn to love that process. Actors spend more time in the preparation of the role (the process) than they do onstage or in front of the camera. The fun should be in the groundwork; then, the ecstasy of performance is inevitable. Training enhances talent and skill, creating artists and performances that are ultimately spellbinding. This philosophy is mirrored in our company, US Performing Arts. With our partner colleges and universities, we introduce young performers to the joy of working in an intensive conservatory-style summer program with like-minded peers under the direction of dedicated professional faculty. It's our feeling that young artists deserve a safe place to explore, develop, and perfect their skills under the tutelage of caring professionals. Through mentoring and encouraging young people to continue their education and training we hope to build future generations of artists and audiences alike.

JUDITH PATTERSON, CEO, US PERFORMING ARTS

But acting classes aren't the only place to act for fun. Use the library or the Internet to look for local opportunities. Audition for children's theatre productions in your community. Be prepared to commit to a long rehearsal period for very few performances. As with school plays and summer camp productions, community theatre is a perfect model to demonstrate that the process is at least as important as the result. You'll work for months on a project to perform it a half a dozen times at most. In some cases, you'll be *double cast*, that is you'll share your role with a friend so that as many kids as possible have a chance to shine. Parents, teachers, directors, and actors themselves agree that community theatre experience can be invaluable and transformational, too.

Interview with Broderick Miller, Artistic Director, The Silverlake Children's Theatre Company, Los Angeles

What makes a kid stand out in an audition?
Poise, confidence, ease on stage—and that intangible sparkle in the eye, genuine smile, spirited bearing. Someone who is enjoying himself and not afraid to show it.

How do you help a child to get over performance jitters?
Building confidence in the rehearsal process. By the time we get to the shows, I have spent one-on-one time with each kid praising her hard work and pointing out how her skillful performance reflects that hard work. Also reinforce the idea—repetitively—about how much fun performances are. The goal is for the kids to eagerly anticipate performances, not dread them.

Is there any mistake you've made in your work with kids?
How much time do you have? Among a multitude of mistakes, the one that is hardest to overcome is miscasting. Once a child gets a role, you can never, never take it away from that kid and give it to someone else. You just have to work that much harder to raise the kid to the level his peers are working on in that particular scene.

Anything you'd do differently next time?

It's always different the "next time." Like the kids, the adults also experience a journey of learning. The most difficult task—but also the most fun—is monitoring the growth/development of talent from year to year and learning to cast/use it wisely. Challenge the actors, but don't put them in a position where they can't deliver (singing a major solo, for example) and thus feel like they have failed. The trick is to give them challenges they can surmount and feel pride in afterwards.

Is there an anecdote you'd like to share about a specific child? Or the work in general?

Specifically: There was a boy actor who was sullen and miserable the first two years he was in our company. Didn't like his roles, didn't like his fellow actors, didn't like the plays. But then something awakened inside him about respect for his peers and commitment to the play and his roles. He changed overnight and is now a leading talent—and citizen—in the group. Now this happens from time to time, but this particular boy specifically credits our theatre group for showing him what camaraderie actually means and the importance of respect—to others and to himself.

Generally: After each play, a frequent comment from the kids goes something like this: "Thank you for this great experience. I really feel that I have found a place where I belong. It's like a family."

The biggest transformation you've witnessed as a director working with children?

Growing confidence in pushing the envelope in our themes and stories, which encourage children to explore culture, politics, and the human condition in increasingly provocative ways.

How do you see this sort of theatre influencing a child's social and intellectual development?

Children at this age (six to seventeen) learn values and leadership skills. By the time they're twenty it's too late. Our program tries to build a sense of values and community in our children—and this is reflected in the themes of our stories: the value of the people you meet in your life; protecting the community; etc. We discuss these themes during the rehearsal process and it becomes a forum for free thought. And I can't expect respect from the kids just because I'm an adult. I have to give respect in order to receive respect.

Do you write differently for kids than you do for adults?

Not much. I take out the swear words and most things that might offend. And then leave in a few, just to keep people honest. But I have found that our sophisticated stories, themes, and dialogue are appreciated by the kids and spur provocative discussions.

If you like to act, don't limit yourself. By all means pursue the project you like best whether it's musical theatre or comedy or drama, but don't decide because you're a kid that anything is off limits. Don't be afraid of dense language, for instance. The bigger the challenge, the greater the rewards all round. You'll be surprised to discover, once you crack the material, that the characters and circumstances in Shakespeare's plays are real and familiar, in spite of his having written them hundreds of years ago.

If there are no opportunities to act... create them. Start your own group! You'll learn organizational and managerial skills as well as providing yourself with an opportunity to act.

TIPS FROM THE PROS

I have worked with kids in my son's schools, doing adaptations of Shakespeare, which are now published through Dramatic Publishing. A few of the kids have gone on to be professional actors. Some decided it was just way too much work and decided to become doctors instead. But most just had a helluva good time for six weeks and will always remember the experience. One boy with a severe reading disability played Iago in *Othello*, and learned the whole part from a tape my husband made for him. His teachers were amazed. His schoolwork improved overnight. Miracles still happen if you leave kids alone with their natural creativity.

NANCY LINEHAN CHARLES, ACTRESS, WRITER, DIRECTOR, AND MOTHER OF ACTOR WILL ROTHHAAR

Who's to say what you're going to be when you "grow up?" Who's to say you have to choose? Hopefully you'll find something—many things—to inspire and challenge you, to make you want to get up in the morning and go to work almost every day. Whatever you decide to do as an adult, your enthusiasm for acting cannot help but enrich your experience, awaken your intellectual curiosity, stretch your imaginative powers, and connect you to the world in ways you never thought possible. Acting, however and wherever you do it, should make everything you try that much more rewarding and that much more fun.

RECOMMENDED READING

Create a Comedy Group and Give Yourself an Acting Career by Diz White, Smith and Kraus, 2006. This is a step-by-step guide on how to employ yourself. It has both craft and business information and the author actually did exactly what the title suggests.

Chapter 11

Post Script, Or A Few Last Words

We were excited about this book from the beginning, but we never imagined what a good time we'd have writing it, how much we'd learn as artists and teachers and students ourselves. The perspectives and experiences of friends and colleagues moved and inspired, delighted and surprised us, and resonated with conviction and passion for the work we all love to do. So here, in conclusion, we present a few more thoughts and stories, advice and confidences from people we know and trust.

To act is to take a journey into the truth of imaginary circumstances; a journey that will lead you to discover the truth about yourself.

DIANE HARDIN, FOUNDER OF
A YOUNG ACTOR'S SPACE, LOS ANGELES

I have one rule in my classroom. "I don't know" is not an acceptable answer. Children tend to immediately go to this response instead of allowing the answer to come to them. The inner growth a child experiences because he can no longer use "I don't know" as a crutch awakens his curiosity and helps to build his confidence. When asked a question—let's say about a choice he made—a child will have to take a few minutes and go deeper to seek the answer. The self-discovery, thanks to this rule, is extraordinary.

While many of my students become professional performers, this is not my primary goal as an acting teacher. From acting, children learn to make eye contact; to think on their feet; to be in the moment without getting distracted; to put all their focus on somebody else; and my favorite, to take full responsibility for their actions.

I recently got a letter from a student, who, out of millions of children in California, was chosen to represent the state at a leadership council in Washington, D.C. She thanked me, because she said it was through her acting classes that she learned how to be a leader. She's only twelve-years-old.

Young actors can learn the skills, heart, compassion, courage, and perseverance it takes to become conscientious leaders in the world.

CONSTANCE TILLOTSON, MANAGER/ACTING TEACHER, STERLING STUDIOS, LOS ANGELES

Although I had my first job at three months, a Lily Tomlin special, I didn't start studying until I was nine-years-old. I've continued to take acting classes because I think they keep your juices flowing.

DAVID FAUSTINO, ACTOR ON *MARRIED WITH CHILDREN*

My words of wisdom re young actors and those who counsel them is to give them space and allowance for their own discoveries, to nurture their ideas and instincts, to require and encourage self-discipline and self-reliance. That should be the basis for all good work for all ages. And when it stops being fun, get out! Life is just too short.

SUANNE SPOKE, ACTRESS, TEACHER

As the mother of a successful child actor and drama coach to several other top young performers, I see many benefits for a youngster in the pursuit of a professional acting career. There is, of course, the sheer fun of make believe, the satisfaction of being chosen for a part, the excitement of collaborating with a cast and crew, travel, money, etc. But a more educational aspect of the work is the opportunity to analyze characters and their motives. Your young actor will gain insight into herself and others. Reading scripts encourages vocabulary-building and reading comprehension, learning lines is good brainwork, and speaking those lines will give your child confidence and poise—lifetime assets.

PAT BRYANT, YOUNG ACTORS' COACH/MANAGER,
MOTHER OF CLARA BRYANT, ACTRESS

Something I've always asked parents when they sought my advice about a child who wants to act, is are you sure this child truly understands what an actor is? I think more and more being an actor is confused with being a celebrity and children especially don't understand that there is a difference.

BOB MCCRACKEN, DIRECTOR, ACTOR, CHILDREN'S ACTING TEACHER

There are legitimate ways to go about starting a career. First give the child at least a few acting lessons. There are many, many wonderful acting coaches for children. Pick a teacher who is fun. If the child loves to act and is eager to go to class, that's a good sign.

As an on-set acting and dialogue coach I have witnessed many parents and their children. Thankfully, most parents have their children's best interest at heart. And lots of acting coaches offer programs for parents, too. Take advantage of all the help you can get. On set, a child must handle himself like a working adult. He can't be cranky, he must deliver a performance, he must do what's asked of him by the producer or director. And he has to have fun.

Usually kids understand and can jump into pretending. If not, you may be able to supply a hint; something from a life experience that can help your child remember the level of emotion the director needs.

A child may be ready to give up his career before his parent. Listen to your child and let it go. This could be the start of a new phase in the child's life, and in the parent's life, too."

JUDY KERR, ACTING AND ON-SET COACH, AUTHOR OF *ACTING IS EVERYTHING*

Let your child lead you. If the kid really wants it, he'll let you know. Put him in school plays and community productions instead of acting classes. It's a better lab. And support the plays but for God's sake don't be a stage mom or dad. Nothing in the world is less attractive. Be an actor yourself if it means that much to you.

NANCY LINEHAN CHARLES, ACTRESS, WRITER, DIRECTOR, AND MOTHER OF ACTOR WILL ROTHHAAR

As actors, we express our "soulfire" (as the man Bob Marley would call it), through a character. We are literally the character's breath, her essence. Unfortunately there are not always opportunities to release your "soul fire" in the business. You don't want to burn yourself from the inside. That's why it's important to have other creative outlets. Get your creative energy released in as many ways as you can so you don't become dependent on any one way. This is important because you don't want to become a desperate actor. As soon as you become desperate, you stop enjoying acting. Your enjoyment of acting as a creative expression is the very thing that will set you free and help you get the job. Take care of what you love, by not depending on it to support you emotionally and financially. Have FUN! People want to be around fun people—so be one. Bon Voyage!

BROOKE DENYSE, ACTRESS

I have been a professional actor since I was six. By that I mean I joined the Screen Actors Guild that year. I was never forced into acting by anyone, and for that reason it's been fun. Pure fun. I get

paid to do it but I do it because it's fun. Always has been. Well...
there've been a few bumps. I'll tell you about one of them,
because I'm proud to say I've survived an actor's nightmare.

I was eleven-years-old and cast as one of three leads in a major
professional production at the Geffen Playhouse in Los Angeles:
David Mamet's *The Cryptogram*. My character's name was John,
who, according to popular opinion, is the playwright himself. At
the end of the play, John walks upstairs with an open knife, appar-
ently to take his own life.

Mamet is a leading American playwright. His plays are genius,
but they contain difficult language with a lot of pauses and "ums"
and "uhs," which Mamet says are essential to performance. The
words and rhythms really do sound like the characters, but seem
nearly impossible to memorize. My mom and dad drilled me end-
lessly on these lines until I wanted to scream. Through the process
of doing a lot of character work, I finally learned the lines perfectly, including every single "um" and "uh."

One night during a performance, I blanked in the middle of a
speech to the woman playing my mother. I couldn't remember
how many "uhs" I'd said, so I just repeated my last line back to
her. She looked at me blankly. I said the line again. It seemed to
trigger nothing in her. Having never slipped up on stage, I hadn't
the faintest idea how to salvage the situation.

I started to sweat. My costume was a heavy flannel robe, with
heavy flannel pajamas causing the sweat to pour down in streams.
I could hear the sound of my dad's breathing in the audience. I sat
totally still, hoping invisibility was a viable option. I looked at my
stage mother. She was shading her eyes in an odd gesture as if to
distance herself from me. She was having no part of this.

I cleared my throat—twice, as I remember it. I knew it was up to
me to save myself and David Mamet's play. My mouth started to
move and I have absolutely no idea what I said, but at least there
was sound on the stage. Maybe I blacked out, but the next thing I
knew I was back in the dressing room and the show was over. It
seemed to me that the pause had lasted ten minutes, but in reality

it only went on about ten seconds; or at least that's what audience members said, though I was suspicious of their compliments that night. My dad, for instance, looked a bit worse for wear. From this nightmare, I learned several things:

1   Learn your "ums" and "uhs" and then learn them again.

2   Try to work with actors who can rescue you in three seconds or less.

3   Do plays with light, summer costuming.

4   Never listen for your dad's reaction in the middle of a performance.

5   Only do hard playwrights once every decade; do CBS sitcoms in between.

And I learned something else: That I have it within me to help myself out of tough situations. And maybe that's the best lesson anyone can ever learn.

WILL ROTHHAAR, ACTOR

Good acting is not age exclusive. There are outstanding performances given by people of seven and seventy.

JAMIE DONNELLY, COACH

TIPS FOR YOUNG ACTORS

From Helene Kvale, actor/director and professor of acting at the University of Connecticut

1   If you love to act, don't give up. The road will be tough and most people can't hack it. By simply staying in the game, you are already ahead. Tenacity is the key.

2 Early on in your career, say YES to any work. Some say you should only accept leading roles in order to be considered legitimate. I say, get the experience now and practice, so that when that leading role comes along, you are ready for it! Work begets work. You never know who you are going to meet or where that small production may end up. Just do it!

3 Having said that, stay away from porn, and ideally commercials for laxatives, tampons, or any other embarrassing products. The casting director will always tell you that the commercial is going to be incredibly tasteful, but ultimately it is your face representing the product. And having a handful of children chanting "It's the Exlax guy" at the mall is perhaps not the best way to impress your date.

4 Diversify. Keep acting, but also write, direct, produce, teach. This will improve your skills and help you to understand different aspects of the business. It will also make you money doing the thing you love, so you can kiss good-bye to waiting tables. (Although that WILL provide you with good writing material!)

5 Know your "type." This is how the business sees you, so accept your type with grace and work with it. Once you are a recognized actor, you can break the rules and play against "type."

6 Have fun. There's nothing worse than seeing a worried actor on stage or screen. Share the love all the way from the audition room to the performance. Audiences will be attracted to you and hey, that means more work for you!

7   Have the courage to accept who you are. Don't try to be like everyone else. You are much more interesting. (Don't forget that "character" actors generally have longer, more diverse career than leading actors.) OK, we all have traits about ourselves that we hate. Be brave and flaunt it! I guarantee that the auditioners and the audience won't see your "flaw," but will see a confident, exciting actor and WANT you.

8   Be professional. Arrive early, be polite, do your job well (no matter how boring), and leave graciously. That is what you are paid for.

9   Buy at least one amazing suit that looks sensational on you. Keep it subtle. But sharp. Use for auditions and interviews or whenever you need to look put together. You will appear successful and appealing. You can be a slouch once you are a star.

10   Then, organize your closet so that you have your audition clothes in one section: cleaned, ironed, and ready for that last minute audition call. Have a variety of styles and bright, "TV colors" (avoid red), so that you aren't scrambling around and getting frustrated at an already stressful time.

11   In interviews stay light and positive. Sure, make 'em laugh, but be true to yourself. Believe it or not, the director desperately wants you to be right for the job. She is not out to humiliate you. Do not talk about money or problems or conflicts. You can sort out all that out AFTER you get the job. For now, you are available and ready to work. Make it simple for them to hire you.

We asked Nicholas Hiegel, a student in the US Performing Arts programs at UCLA, to tell us why he'd decided to be an actor. Nick had just heard Sanford Meisner's definition of acting for the first time. "If I couldn't act," he said, "If I couldn't live truthfully under the imaginary circumstances, I'd feel imaginary under the truthful ones." Acting is what allows Nick to use his best self most fully; otherwise he feels less present, less real, less alive.

Be like Nick; do it for fun, do it for money, and always, always do it for love.

We can be reached at our website ActingforYoungActors.com or through our publisher:

Watson-Guptill Publications,
770 Broadway, New York, New York 10003
www.watsonguptill.com

Glossary

Action- The verb you use to define how to get what you want in the scene; the intention.

As if- Making believe. Using your imagination to truthfully place yourself in a made-up situation.

At stake- What is at risk if an actor does not fulfill his objective. The circumstances which ground the actor in an emotional situation.

Bank hours- To accomplish extra school hours to ease the load on long shooting days.

Blocking- Staging.

Callback- A second audition for the same role.

Character actor- An artist who plays all kinds of parts and who can't be pegged or defined by one role or another. Not a leading man or leading woman.

Close-up- A camera shot of an actor's head and shoulders.

Cold reading- An audition for which the actor did not receive the material (or sides) ahead of time.

Coogan Trust Account- A bank account named after Jackie Coogan to protect the earnings of minors.

Credits- Previous stage, film, and television experiences listed on a resume.

Double cast- When two performers share the same role, performing it at different performances.

Dramatis personae- The list of characters in the cast which usually appears at the beginning of a play.

Filling in the blanks- Providing yourself with information, actual or made up, that will help you inhabit a role.

Fourth wall- The imaginary wall separating the players from the audience.

Freeze performance- To lock in choices and blocking during a rehearsal period in order to fulfill the director's vision and provide stability and consistency for the actors and the stage crew.

Green screen- A green or blue screen which is placed behind the actor and then replaced by a back plate or other film effect in post-production.

Grip- A crew member who moves electrical equipment or set pieces.

Headshot- An 8" by 10" photograph that you bring along and leave behind at auditions.

In character- Sustaining the physical and emotional qualities of a role that are necessary for a performance.

Independent activity- The physical

activity which may or may not be connected to the actor's objectives and intentions in a scene.

Indicate- To show your intentions and reactions rather than to be in character and to behave "as if."

Ingenue- The young, attractive female role.

Intention- The verb you use to define how to get what you want in the scene; the action.

Justify- To make sense of your character's behavior with specific and personal details.

Juvenile lead- The young, attractive male role.

Line reading- When an actor is asked to imitate a spoken line or word without exploring intentions or objectives on his own. An inorganic way of eliciting a performance with results rather than process in mind.

Location- An actual place rented by a production company for use in a film or TV show.

Master- A camera shot that holds all the principle actors in a scene.

Moment to moment- The idea that good acting is reacting and staying present, so that each moment is based on the one immediately prior.

Monologue- A long speech delivered by a single character in a play, movie, or TV show.

Objective- What you want in the scene especially as it relates to the other person in the scene.

Obstacle- Any impediment to getting what you want in a scene.

Off-book- Knowing your lines by heart, so that you do not need to rely on the script.

One-person show- A show with a cast of one.

Packing- Accumulating personal and historical details to help an actor to access a role.

Pad- To add credits to your resume, in some cases, for work you didn't actually do. Lengthening a scene by adding words not written by the author.

Period piece- A theatrical piece that takes place in another time, usually in the past.

Personalizing- Identifying specific details that you have in common with the character you're playing.

Placing your partner in the room- An audition technique for monologues in which an actor imagines the other character is standing within his fourth wall.

POV- (point of view) - A camera angle description referring to the character's physical frame of reference.

Pre-read- An audition with a casting director designed to determine whether or not an actor will read for producers.

Preparation- Anything an actor does to get into character.

Raise the stakes- To make the circumstances more important to your character.

Read between the lines- To interpret information by considering the point of view of the person saying it. Piecing together the clues in a script.

Repetition- A method exercise devised by teacher Sanford Meisner to help actors to discover their impulses and act truthfully from moment to moment regardless of the words they are speaking.

Resume - A list of credits. Usually stapled to the back of a headshot.

Set- The scenery.

Sides- The pages of the selected scene(s) to be read at an audition.

Soliloquy- A monologue in which the character is talking to himself.

Sound Stage- A large airplane hanger-like structure which can be filled with sets for production.

Substitution- Using a circumstance from your own experience or imagination to help you relate to the circumstances of the script. Acting "as if."

Subtext- A character's unspoken thoughts and intentions.

Table read- A reading of the scenes in a script in consecutive order before a rehearsal period begins.

Taft Hartley Law- A law that requires actors to join labor unions.

Triple Threat- A performer who is equally proficient at acting, singing, and dancing.

Two-shot- A description for a camera shot that holds two actors.

Up tempo- A rhythmic, fast paced song.

Ying Yang- The Chinese symbol for opposing yet complementary forces. An improvisational exercise used by Manuel Duque while at Penn State to show that conflict is based on characters wanting opposite things. The exercise is designed to help actors get in touch with playing their objectives.

Unions and Professional Organizations

Screen Actors Guild (SAG)
Labor organization representing actors in feature films, television, short films, and digital projects.
www.sag.org

Los Angeles
5757 Wilshire Blvd.
Los Angeles, CA 90036
(323) 954-1600

New York
360 Madison Ave., 12th Fl.
New York City, NY 10017
(212) 944-1030

American Federation of Television and Radio Artists (AFTRA)
Labor organization representing actors in television and radio broadcasts.
www.aftra.org

Los Angeles
5757 Wilshire Blvd., Suite 900
Los Angeles, CA 90036
(323) 634-8100

New York
260 Madison Ave., 7th Fl.
New York, NY 10016
(212) 532-0800

Casting Society of America
An honorary society of casting directors. To be admitted, one
must first apply and then be voted on.
www.castingsociety.com
606 N. Larchmont Blvd., Suite 4B
Los Angeles, CA 90004
(323) 463-1925

Association of Talent Agents/ATA
Nonprofit trade association for talent agencies.
www.agentassociation.com
9255 Sunset Blvd.
Los Angeles , CA 90069
(310) 274-0628

Talent Managers Association/TMA
Nonprofit organization that promotes the highest standards of
professionalism in the practice of talent management.
www.talentmanagers.org
4804 Laurel Canyon Blvd., #611
Valley Village, CA 91607
(310) 205-8495

Resources and Services

A Minor Consideration
A nonprofit organization that aids and supports young entertainers.
www.minorcon.org/tenyearstime.html

14530 Denker Ave.
Gardena, CA 90247
(310) 523-3691 (fax)

Actors' Work Program
Career counseling for members of the Actors' Fund of America.
www.actorsfund.org

Los Angeles
5757 Wilshire Blvd., Suite 400
Los Angeles, CA 90036-3635
(323) 933-9244

New York
729 Seventh Ave., 11th Fl.
New York, NY 10019
(212) 354-5480

ABC Talent Development Programs
ABC and Touchstone are equal-opportunity employers with a
long history of identifying and offering opportunities to
culturally and ethnically diverse talent.
www.abctalentdevelopment.com

500 S Buena Vista St.
Burbank, CA 91521-4395
(818) 460-6055

Breakdown Services Ltd.
Communications network and casting system that provides
integrated tools for casting directors, talent agents, and managers,
as well as essential information for actors.
www.breadownservices.com

Los Angeles   (310) 276-9166

New York   (212) 869-2003

Vancouver   (604) 943-7100

London: (20) 7437-7631

Libraries and Bookstores Specializing in Performing Arts Collections

(If you can't find the books and plays we've recommended at your local library, Amazon.com, or your local bookstore, you'll be sure to find them at the places listed below.)

Samuel French, Inc.
Publishers of plays. Terrific resource for plays and performing arts books. www.samuelfrench.com

Los Angeles
7623 Sunset Blvd.
Hollywood, CA 90046
(323) 876-0570

11963 Ventura Blvd.
Studio City, CA 91604
(818) 762-0535

New York
45 W. 25th St.
New York City, NY 10036
(212) 206-8990

Drama Book Shop
A wonderful bookstore for industry trade books and plays.
www.dramabookshop.com

250 W. 40th St.
New York, NY 10018
(212) 944-0595

American Film Institute
Organization dedicated to preserving and advancing the art of the
moving image through special events, exhibitions, and education.
The library is open to public for in-house use.
www.afi.com

Los Angeles
2021 N. Western Ave.
Los Angeles, CA 90027
(323) 856-7600

Washington, D.C.
The John F. Kennedy Center for the Performing Arts
(202) 833-2348

Academy of Motion Picture Arts and Sciences—
Margaret Herrick Library
Research and reference collection.
www.oscars.org

333 S. La Cienega Blvd.
Beverly Hills, CA 90211
(310) 247-3035

Los Angeles Public Library—
Frances Howard Goldwyn/Hollywood Regional Branch Library
www.LAPL.org

Special Entertainment Industry Collection
1623 N. Ivar Ave.
Los Angeles, CA 90028
(323) 856-8260

Museum of Television and Radio
Extensive collection of television and radio programming.
www.mtr.org

Los Angeles
465 N. Beverly Dr.
Beverly Hills, CA 90210
(310) 786-1000

New York
25 W. 52nd St.
New York, NY 10019
(212) 621-6600

New York Public Library for Performing Arts
Extensive combination of circulating, reference, and rare archival
collections in the performing arts.
www.nypl.org

40 Lincoln Center Plaza
New York, NY 10019
(212) 621-6600

UCLA Arts Library

Excellent resource material including special script collections.
www.library.ucla.edu

1400 Public Policy Bldg.
Los Angeles, CA 90095
(310) 206-5425

Writers Guild Foundation—James R. Webb Memorial Library

Collection dedicated to the art, craft, and history of writing for
motion pictures, radio, television, and new media. Open to the
public and Guild members.

7000 W. Third St.
Los Angeles, CA 90048-4329
(323) 782-4544

Dramatists Play Service Inc.

Play publisher.
www.dramatists.com

440 Park Ave. So.
New York, NY 10016
(212) 683-8960

Recommended Classes

A Young Actors Space
(818) 785-7979
www.youngactorsspace.com
For twenty-five years, this school has provided unique and
exciting training for actors from age four to adults. The founder,
Diane Hill Hardin, has been a vital force in young actors' lives in
Los Angeles. She teaches master classes as well in New York City.

Acting For REAL
Suanne Spoke
Call Donne McRae (818) 243-5182 (office) or (818) 618-5857
(cell) www.suannespoke.com
An award-winning actor/producer/coach, Spoke produced and
starred in the critically-acclaimed *Napoli Milionaria* at the Road
Theatre, for which she won an Ovation Award for Best Actress
and a Los Angeles Drama Critics' Award for Best Production. She
has been coaching privately for over seven years while also
cultivating her own TV and film career, guest starring on over one
hundred TV shows. Her class is geared toward the specific needs
of the individual, focusing on character development, expanding
one's instrument, and script analysis. Classes run in ten-week
sessions (in the NOHO arts district) which include working

seminars with casting directors, producers, and directors.
Preliminary interviews are required and auditing is available.

Catlin Adams Acting Lab
(323)851-8811
An award-winning director and actress, Adams teaches an all
levels class on Monday nights at the Hudson Avenue Theatre in
Hollywood. Classes cover improvisation, sensory work, camera
technique exercises, monologue, and scene study. All classes are
taught by Adams herself. Learn to prepare for a part, create a
character, break down a script, and become your own director.
Students work in every class. Class size is strictly limited.

Joel Asher Studio
(818) 785-1551
www.Joel-Asher-Studio.com.
Joel Asher, who has been teaching and directing for over thirty
years, offers three ongoing on-camera scene study classes, a cold
reading class, and an improvisation class. These are classes
for motivated actors who are treated as adults. Class size is limited
so everyone participates in every class. "I also work with actors in
between classes at no charge," says Asher. "There are no limits to
the time you can spend learning and doing, getting help with
your career, or the techniques we use to get results." Joel Asher's
Studio in Sherman Oaks produced the award-winning *Actors At
Work* video series and also creates state-of-the-art demo reels for
actors.

the barn...scene study and workshops with John Short
(323) 610-6560
Scene study at the barn is not about having all the answers. It is
about knowing what questions to ask regarding your character
and the requirements of the scene. Who am I? What do I want?
How am I going to get it? How you answer these fundamental
questions determines your unique vision of the character. That

vision, combined with the ability to make your scene partner more important than you, is the key to creating work on stage or screen that has nothing to do with "good" acting, and everything to do with being present and alive in your work.

Scene study classes and special workshops are taught by veteran actor and teacher John Short, whose credits run the gamut from the Broadway stage to feature films. Auditing is free and highly encouraged.

Creative City Repertory Co.
(310) 657-6446
Martha Melinda teaches long form comedy improvisation in a cozy setting. She touches on current issues that appeal to kids. Melinda gets kids and they adore her!

Howard Fine Acting Studio
(323) 951-1174
www.howardfine.com
Instructors at the studio include Fine, Marilyn McIntyre, as well as other highly qualified acting teachers.

The Laura Henry Acting Studio
(310) 399-5744
Founded in 1992, Henry directs this training program for beginning and advanced actors. Classes offered include short term courses as well as a two year conservatory program. Henry teaches Meisner technique, audition technique, as well as other classes. Graduates include Keiko Agena from *Gilmore Girls*, and Mike O'Malley from *Yes, Dear.*

Improv for Actors
(818) 769-3767
Taught by actor Jeff Doucette.

Harvey Lembeck Comedy Workshop
Helaine Lembeck, Michael Lembeck
(310) 271-2831
Now in its fortieth year, the workshop has three levels aimed at
the trained/working actor who wants to specialize in comedy. The
workshop is designed to teach the actor how to play comedy
legitimately in a scene, and uses improv as a tool to enhance the
comedic skills for sitcoms, TV, and film. The student participates
on stage three to four times each night. An interview and an
audition is required for these ongoing classes. Critiques are by the
teacher only. The classes are often made up of professionals from
all areas of the industry. Former students include Robin Williams,
Penny Marshall, John Ritter, Jenna Elfman, Bryan Cranston, Kim
Cattrall, John Laroquette, Alan Rachins, and Sharon Stone.

Louder! Faster! Funnier! Sitcom Techniques Class
(818) 991-6911   E-mail: phil@louderfasterfunnier.com
Class taught by Phil Ramuno, co-author with Mary Lou Belli of
The Sitcom Career Book.

Sharron Madden's Class
(323) 655-3795
Madden was a founding member of Circle Repertory Company.
She teaches children's theatre workshop at the Interact Theater
Company in L.A. Her private adult class includes scenes from
TV/film, cold reading, and camera technique making choices.
She helps actors face their struggle to keep creativity and
concentration alive during auditions.

Scott Sedita Acting Studio
(323) 465-6152   www.scottseditaacting.com
Scott Sedita, recently seen as the resident acting coach on the E!
series *Fight For Fame*, has years of experience in both New York
and Los Angeles as an agent, casting director, and acting coach.

He has worked with many of today's most successful television and film actors and continues to groom future stars through his studio.

Recommended
Acting Coaches

Catlin Adams (323) 851-8811
Private Coaching (see Catlin Adams Acting Lab under
Recommended Acting Classes).

Joel Asher (818) 785-1551
(See Joel Asher Studio under Recommended Acting Classes.)

Jamie Donnelly
Jamiedonnelly@mac.com
On-set and private coaching.

Denise Dowse (323) 369-9582
poohzly@aol.com
Working actress who offers private coaching sessions for auditions, has been on-set dialog/acting coach for numerous series,
teaches an ongoing Adult Acting Class and is the Resident
Director at Amazing Grace Conservatory (AGC), a Performing
Arts School for youth ages six to twenty-one. Client list is vast and
varied.

Judy Kain
TALENT TO GO ... We Deliver!
(818) 901-8606

www.talenttogo.net
This is a unique approach to coaching and showcasing. Actors of
all ages rehearse three-minute scenes with Kain, then do them for
directors, producers, and casting people. It is quick, fun, and
reasonable.

Judy Kerr
(818) 505-9373
Judykerr.com or actingiseverything.com
On-set and private coaching, one-time sessions for career
coaching.

Sharon Madden
(323) 665-3795
On-set and private coaching. Wonderful with young talent.

Art Manke
(323) 667-1231.
Private coach. Manke has over twenty years of experience as an
actor, director, and coach. In addition to directing numerous
award-winning productions across the country, he was a founding
artistic director of L.A.'s acclaimed classical theatre company, A
Noise Within, and was trained at the prestigious American
Conservatory Theatre.

Steve Muscarella
(818) 789-6898
muscarella@earthlink.net
On-set and off-set coaching. Helps actors with scenes and monologues as well as showcase preparation.

Dinah Lenney
(323) 664-8186
Private coach for adults and children for theater, television, and
film auditions.

Phil. Ramuno
(818) 991-6911
www.louderfasterfunnier.com

Scott Sedita
See Scott Sedita Acting Studio
(323) 465-6152
www.scottseditaacting.com

Suanne Spoke
(818) 487-1860
Private Coaching (see Acting for REAL under Recommended
Acting Classes).

Kitty Swink
(818) 508-9169
On-set and private coaching. Wonderful with young talent.

Mark Taylor
(818) 786-5712
On-set and private coaching. Comedy and drama.

Fred Tucker
(310) 413-4605
Freddvision@msn.com
Award-winning stage actor with television and film acting credits
as well. Private coaching list includes many standup comedians.
Scene study and improv teacher. Presently dialolgue and acting
coach for UPN Sitcom *Cuts.*

Recommended Publications

Hollywood Creative Directory/HCD
Comprehensive list of contact information for TV and film industry. We highly recommend having this resource in your personal library.
www.hcdonline.com
1024 N. Orange Dr.
Hollywood, CA 90038
(323) 308-3400
(800) 815-0530

Ross Reports Television and Film
Listing of agents and casting director contact information.
770 Broadway
New York, NY 10003
(646) 654-5730 (editorials)
(800) 745-8922 (subscription)

Back Stage
Industry trade publication (NY). Has best theatre information for actors.
www.backstage.com
770 Broadway
New York, NY 10003
(646) 654-5700

Back Stage West
Industry trade publication (L.A.). Has best theatre information for actors.
www.backstage.com
5055 Wilshire Blvd.
Los Angeles, CA 90036-6100
(323) 525-2358

Academy Players Directory
www.playersdirectory.com
Print and online casting
directories. Most actors have their
photo in this directory.
1313 N. Vine St.
Hollywood CA 90028
(310) 247-3058

Daily Variety
Known as one of the trade papers
or "trades."
www.variety.com
Los Angeles
5700 Wilshire Blvd., Suite 120
Los Angeles, CA 90036
(323) 857-6600
New York
(646) 746-7002

Hollywood Reporter
Known as one of the trade papers
or "trades."
www.hollywoodreporter.com
5055 Wilshire Blvd., 6th Fl.
Los Angeles, CA 90036
(323) 525-2000

*Directory of Theatre Training
Programs, 9th edition*
The complete guide of available
graduate and undergraduate
programs in the U.S. and other
countries as well. Available
through Samuel French
Bookstore.

Recommended Books

The Sitcom Career Book by Mary Lou Belli and Phil Ramuno, Back Stage Books, 2004. The best and only book of its kind. Everything you need to know about acting on a sitcom.

The Actors Encyclopedia of Casting Directors by Karen Kondazian, Lone Eagle Publishing Co., 2000. Kondazian has compiled insider information and intimate profiles from talking to premiere casting directors in film, television, theatre, and commercials from Los Angeles to New York.

The Actor's Handbook by Sherry Eaker, Back Stage Books, 2004. Practical and handy guide if you are pursuing acting professionally.

Acting Is Everything: An Actor's Guide Book for a Successful Career in Los Angeles by Judy Kerr, September Publishing 2003. Kerr's personal reference guide from her thirty years as an L.A. acting coach, now in its eighth edition.

The Audition Book by Ed Hooks, Back Stage Books, 2000. Gems from a master.

The Actor's Field Guide: Acting Notes on the Run by Ed Hooks, Back Stage Books, 2004. Anecdotal and helpful info for craft and career. A fun read!

How to Audition by Gordon Hunt, Quill, Harper Collins, 1995. A terrific guide from a wonderful director of theatre and television.

Book on Acting: Improvisation Technique by Stephen Book, Silmar-James Press, 2002. Book's unique approach is for the more advanced actor.

Improv Comedy by Andy Goldberg, Samuel French Trade, 1992. The best book on improv. Great fun to read.

Sanford Meisner on Acting by Sanford Meisner and Dennis Longwell, Vintage, Random House, 1987. A book from one of the great acting teachers of all time.

Next: An Actor's Guide to Auditioning by Ellie Kanner, C.S.A. & Paul G. Bens Jr., Lone Eagle Publishing Co. 1997. Advice from casting directors who know.

Auditioning by Joanna Merlin, Vintage, Random House, 2001. Advice from a casting director with long, distinguished career.

The Art of Acting by Stella Adler, Applause Books, 2000. A classic from one of the great acting teachers of all time.

Audition by Michael Shurtlleff, Bantam Books, 1980. Required reading for professional actors.

Respect For Acting by Uta Hagen, Wiley Publishing, Inc., 1973. A practical approach to acting from one of the great acting teachers of all time.

Challenge for the Actor by Uta Hagen, Simon and Schuster, Inc., 1991. A great sequel to her first book from one of the finest actresses and teachers of her generation.

On the Technique of Acting by Michael Chekov, HarperCollins, Inc., 1991. Dated yet still appropriate.

Acting in Film by Michael Caine, Applause Theatre Books, 2000. Advice from one of the greats.

Acting: The First Six Lessons by Richard Boleslavsky, Theatre Arts, Inc. 1994. This short book on acting is a gem. Although it is older than most of the texts we recommend, the simple wisdom holds true.

Tips by Jon Jory, Smith & Kraus, 2000. Jory put the Actors Theatre of Louisville on the map. A great man of the theatre.

Cold Reading and How To Be Good At It by Basil Hoffman, Dramaline Publications, 1999. Great advice from one who has been there, done it and taught it!

Plays, Players and Playwrights by Marion Geisinger, Hart Publishing Co., 1971. A great reference book for any theatre library.

The Eight Characters of Comedy by Scott Sedita, Atides Publishing, 2005. A unique approach. A must for anyone who wants to do comedy.

The Working Actor's Toolkit by Jean Schiffman, Heinemann, 2003. Some great interviews with pros.

From Agent to Actor by Edgar Small, Samuel French Trade, 1999. Practical professional advice.

The Art of Auditioning by Rob Decina, Allworth Press, 2004. Especially helpful for musicals.

Acting With an Accent by David Alan Stern. Tips from the best authority on accents. Individuals tapes for accents available through Samuel French.

Recommended Plays

Broadway by George Abbott

The Goat by Edward Albee

Five Tall Women by Edward Albee

The Baby Dance by Jane Anderson

Mary of Scotland by Maxwell Anderson

Tea and Sympathy by Robert Anderson

The Lark by Jean Anouilh adapted by Lillian Hellman

Thieves Carnival by Jean Anouilh

Intimate Exchanges by Alan Ayckbourn

Relatively Speaking by Alan Ayckbourn

Kid Champion by Thomas Babe

The Real Queen of Hearts Ain't Even Pretty by Brad Bailey

The Film Society by Jon Robin Baitz

Red Noses by Peter Barnes

The Admirable Crichton by James M. Barrie

Holiday by Philip Barry

The Philadelphia Story by Philip Barry

Endgame by Samuel Beckett

A Walk in the Woods by Lee Blessing

Mother Courage by Bertolt Brecht

Life in the Trees by Catherine Butterfield

The Balcony Scene by Will Calhoun

Love of a Pig by Leslie Caveny

Anne of Green Gables by Alice Chadwicke

Middle of the Night by Paddy Chayefsky

Three Sisters by Anton Chekhov

The Cherry Orchard by Anton Chekhov

The Seagull by Anton Chekhov

Cloud 9 by Caryl Churchill

Top Girls by Caryl Churchill

Merton of the Movies by George S. Kaufmann and Marc Connelly

Hay Fever by Noel Coward

Private Lives by Noel Coward

A Quarrel of Sparrows by James Duff

Beyond Therapy by Christopher Durang

Nicholas Nickleby by David Edgar (adaptation)

Widows and Children First by Harvey Fierstein

Chemical Reactions by Andy Foster

Noises Off by Michael Frayn

Lovers by Brian Friel

Translations by Brian Friel

Master Harold and the Boys by Athol Fugard

A Soldier's Play by Charles Fuller

I'm Not Rappaport by Herb Gardner

Butterflies Are Free by Leonard Gershe

The Miracle Worker by William Gibson

The Only Game in Town by Frank Gilroy

The Inspector General by Nickolai Gogol

The Servant of Two Masters by Carlo Goldoni

Otherwise Engaged by Simon Grey

Six Degrees of Separation by John Guare

House of Blue Leaves by John Guare

Love Letters by A.R. Gurney

Scenes from American Life by A.R. Gurney

Les Liasons Dangereuses by Christopher Hampton

A Raisin In the Sun by Lorraine Hansberry

Amy's View by David Hare

Skylight by David Hare

Turn Back the Clock by Marrijane Hayes and Joseph Hayes

The Front Page by Ben Hecht

Crimes of the Heart by Beth Henley

The Miss Firecracker Contest by Beth Henley

Blue Denim by James Herlihy and William Noble

My Old Lady by Israel Horowitz

Morning Noon and Night by Israel Horowitz

Painting Churches by Tina Howe

M. Butterfly by David Henry Hwang

Hedda Gabler by Henrik Ibsen

The Wild Duck by Henrik Ibsen

Rhinoceros by Eugene Ionesco

The Texas Trilogy by Preston Jones

The Royal Family by George S. Kaufmann and Edna Ferber

Wings by Arthur Kopit

Angels in America by Tony Kushner

The Shape of Things by Neil LaBute

Table Settings by James Lapine

Da by Hugh Leonard

Veronica's Room by Ira Levin

The House of Bernarda Alba by Federico Garcia Lorca

The Belle of Amherst by William Luce

The Cook by Eduardo Machado

The Frog Prince by David Mamet

Sexual Perversity in Chicago by David Mamet

American Buffalo by David Mamet

Keely and Du by Jane Martin

Picasso at the Lapin Agile by Steve Martin

The Woolgatherer by William Mastrosimone

Someone Who'll Watch Over Me by Frank McGuiness

Modigliani by Dennis McIntyre

Noon by Terrence McNally

Night by Leonard Melfi

The Crucible by Arthur Miller

Death of a Salesman by Arthur Miller

A View from the Bridge by Arthur Miller

Tartuffe by Moliere

All the Way Home by Tad Mosel

Joe Egg by Peter Nichols

Shadowlands by William Nicholson

Quint and Miss Jessel at Bly by Don Nigro

Away Alone by Janet Noble

Last Dance by Marsha Norman

Once a Catholic by Mary O'Malley

Long Days Journey Into Night by Eugene O'Neill

Entertaining Mr. Sloan by Joe Orton

Morning's At Seven by Paul Osborne

Sorrows of Stephen by Peter Parnell

Roman Conquest by John Patrick

Kennedy's Children by Robert Patrick

Penguin Blues by Ethan Phillips

Agnes of God by John Pielmeier

The Homecoming by Harold Pinter

Six Characters in Search of an Author by Luigi Pirandello

Hurlyburly by David Rabe

Separate Tables by Terence Rattigan

Spike Heels by Theresa Rebeck

Street Scene by Elmer Rice

Twelve Angry Men by Reginald Rose

Educating Rita by Willy Russell

Crossing Delancey by Susan Sandler

The Time of Your Life by William Saroyan

Sleuth by Anthony Shaffer

Equus by Peter Shaffer

Romeo and Juliet by William Shakespeare

The Tempest by William Shakespeare

Doubt by John Patrick Shanley

Pygmalion by George Bernard Shaw

Saint Joan by George Bernard Shaw

True West by Sam Shepard

Buried Child by Sam Shepard

Bent by Martin Sherman

Daddy's Dyin' by Del Shores

Story Theatre by Paul Sills

Correct Address by Judd Silverman

Barefoot in the Park by Neil Simon

The Gingerbread Lady by Neil Simon

I Ought to Be in Pictures by Neil Simon

I Remember You by Bernard Slade

I Capture the Castle by Dodie Smith

Antigone by Sophocles

A Few Good Men by Aaron Sorkin

Making Movies by Aaron Sorkin

The Runner Stumbles by Milan Stitt

The Real Thing by Tom Stoppard

Rosencrantz and Guildenstern Are Dead by Tom Stoppard

The Changing Room by David Storey

Fortune's Fools by Fredrick Stroppel

The Haggadah by Elizabeth Swados

Bluff by Jeffrey Sweet

Porch by Jeffrey Sweet

The Playboy of the Western World by J.M. Synge

Pot Mom by Justin Tanner

Zombie Attack! by Justin Tanner

The Trysting Place by Booth Tarkington

Lovers and Other Strangers by Renee Taylor

Approaching Simone by Megan Terry

On the Open Road by Steve Tesich

A Month In the Country by Ivan Turgenev

Confession of a Dirty Blonde by Billy Van Zandt and Jane Milmore

Happy Birthday Wanda June by Kurt Vonnegut, Jr.

Key Exchange by Kevin Wade

The Search for Signs of Intelligent Life In the Universe by Jane Wagner

Third by Wendy Wasserstein

Uncommon Women and Others by Wendy Wasserstein

Loose Ends by Michael Weller

The Importance of Being Earnest by Oscar Wilde

Our Town by Thorton Wilder

The Glass Menagerie by Tennessee Williams

A Streetcar Named Desire by Tennessee Williams

Sweet Bird of Youth by Tennessee Williams

The Piano Lesson by August Wilson

The Fifth of July by Lanford Wilson

Fighting Light by Greg Zittel

Index

L

M

N

O

P

T

U

ABOUT THE AUTHORS

Emmy Award–winning Mary Lou Belli currently directs UPN's hit sitcom *Eve* starring the Grammy and MTV award–winning hip-hop artist of the same name, *Living With Fran* starring Fran Drescher, and *Misconceptions* starring Jane Leeves. After receiving a BA in theatre from Penn State, Mary Lou acted in musical theatre and soaps in New York, and then moved to Los Angeles where she began producing and directing theatre. Her directing career in television started with multiple episodes of *Charles In Charge* , *Major Dad*, *The Hughleys*, and *Sister, Sister*, and continues with such current shows as *Girlfriends*, and *One on One*, for which she was honored by a nomination for Best Directing Team by Black Entertainment Television. Mary Lou is known for her work in children's programming—she coached on NBC's Saturday morning hit *Saved by the Bell: The New Class* and went on to direct *USA High*, *One World*, Nickelodeon's *Amber, Amber*, and Fox's teenage soap opera, *Tribes*. She is currently at work developing the movie *No Daughter of Mine* for Lifetime Television. Among her many awards, her favorite is the citation from former Los Angeles Mayor Tom Bradley for her work with abused children. She lives with her actor husband, Charles Dougherty, and their two children.

Dinah Lenney received her BA from Yale and a Certificate of Acting from the Neighborhood Playhouse where she studied with Sanford Meisner. She holds an MFA in Creative Nonfiction from the Bennington Writing Seminars and her essays appear in national journals, anthologies, and newspapers. Dinah's acted up and down both coasts and continues to work in theatre, film, and television. She's played Nurse Shirley on NBC's critically acclaimed *ER* for twelve seasons and was honored by the Screen Actors Guild as a member of the Best Ensemble in 1997. Dinah coaches privately and works as an adjunct professor for performing arts programs at University of California, Los ngeles; University of California, San Diego; and Pepperdine University. In spring of '07 The University of Nebraska Press will publish her memoir as of their continuing series, "American Lives." Dinah lives in Los Angeles 'er husband, Fred, and their children, Eliza and Jake